The Decorative Art of
Dried Flower
Arrangement

The Decorative Art of Dried Flower Arrangement

GEORGIA S. VANCE

1972

Doubleday & Company, Inc., Garden City, New York

Acknowledgments

My sincere thanks are extended to my family and friends for their interest and co-operation: to my husband for his patience and encouragement; to my sister for her generous help both in the preparation of this book and in the dried flower project; to the other Georgia, Mrs. Jack C. Fuson, for a happy association in creating our decorative style of dried flower arrangement.

Many others have given help, but I am particularly grateful to Dr. Elizabeth B. Johnson for identification of plant species and other generous assistance; to Mr. Kenneth L. Bergeron for his patient and painstaking photography; to my friends who created arrangements for this book, one of whom, Mrs. Paul E. Todd, was my consultant on Ikebana; to Brigadier S. E. M. Goodall for his efforts in locating books on eighteenth-century flower painting and to Dr. Santina P. Bayerle for her translation of *Flora*.

To Mr. Clement E. Conger, Chairman, Special Fine Arts Committee, Department of State, my appreciation for his advice on the Federal Period, and to his staff and the staff of Gunston Hall for their co-operation; and, finally, to Mrs. Christine Shank Robins for help in getting this project underway.

Contents

ILLUSTRATIONS

Color (follows pages 50 and 130)

"Veiled Bouquet" by Hobson Pittman. In the collection of The Corcoran Gallery of Art.

Introduction: Artist or Craftsman?

The craftsman as such is not an artist. The good craftsman constructs his product as perfectly as he can, he takes faithfully the steps necessary to that end. He becomes an artist insofar as he treats his materials also for themselves, and the craftsman may be and is perpetually besieged by dreams of beauty in his work. From skill he proceeds to good taste and from taste to charm and beauty.

Beauty and Other Forms of Value, by S. Alexander.

May this book be for the beginner an invitation and introduction to the history, techniques and possibilities of this old but ever-new art. For the already initiated, perhaps a new perspective may be offered.

Although dried flowers have provided winter bouquets for centuries, arrangers today are fascinated with exceptional dried plant material for arrangements of all styles.

To capture the characteristic form of a blossom at its loveliest stage of development, and yet to have it possess new attributes and new charm as a dried flower, is an exciting accomplishment. Flowers have such a fascination: Greater appreciation and awareness of their artistic potentialities and limitations are gained through an intimate association with them in the craft of preservation and the art of arranging.

Flowers from the garden, the field and the florist can be dried to possess distinctive qualities. They may be brightly colorful to display their original hues, or again, they may become exotics with intriguing changes in color.

Since the substance, texture, fragility, color and structure of flowers differ so widely, various methods and techniques of preservation are required. There can be no one best method for preserving all plant material, nor can all kinds be preserved.

Advanced techniques in the use of ancient, as well as newly discovered methods are described in detail, and specific procedures, based on trial and error, are recommended. By faithfully taking the steps necessary, skill in this craft can be easily acquired.

In creating dried flower arrangements, one finds that originality and creativity are the outgrowth of craft—that good craftsmanship is the prerequisite of artistry. Not every arrangement need be a work of art: Imaginative, decorative designs to enhance the decor also satisfy the "dreams of beauty" we all experience.

The traditions of flower arrangement in various historical periods in Italy, Holland and Flanders, France, England, Japan and in our own country reflect the tastes, temperament and fashions of the time.

Works of famous artists since the Renaissance period, reproduced in this book, are high points in the development of this art and have greatly influenced contemporary flower arrangement.

Photographs of the dried arrangements demonstrate the versatility of preserved plant material and its use in creating traditional decorative styles and also designs in the latest fashion—a break with tradition.

Part One

CREATING
DRIED FLOWER ARRANGEMENTS
FOR ANY DECOR

1 The Styles of Flower Arrangement Through History

Styles, fashions and tastes in flower arrangement, as in all art, are ever-changing. Only the values set by art are constant. Awareness of beauty comes through what the artist makes visible, and art reflects the whole manner of life of a people or a period.

The traditions of flower arrangement of both East and West are seen through the eyes of artists in flower paintings, prints, etchings and tapestries, and in the work of the artists and skilled craftsmen of the decorative arts. They have also been described in literature.

During the Renaissance period in Italy (1400–1600), man became aware again of the beauty of ancient Rome which had in turn been developed from the Greek. The classic style of ancient Greece was aimed at perfection of symmetry and rhythm beyond the reach of nature. When forms were borrowed from nature they were fashioned into a stylized formula representing the ideal type of this form. How perfectly flowers and foliage composed as wreaths, garlands and swags fit the formula!

In this period of the "great awakening" and "revival of learning" there was recognition and acceptance of humanism. Flowers, however, appeared as symbols, for painting still belonged to the church. During the High Renaissance, the individualism and freedom expressed in the works of the great masters, Michelangelo, da Vinci and Raphael led toward the development of the baroque style.

The term "baroque" describes the tendencies prevailing in the art of the sixteenth, seventeenth and eighteenth centuries. From its beginning in Italy the style swept Europe and spread to the New World. It was characterized by a sense of movement and an appeal to the emotions.

One salient feature of the irregular rhythmic movement is the S-curve, called by William Hogarth, the great English painter, "the line of beauty." Artists imparted a special character of their own to baroque—a character to suit the tastes and temperament of the country. It was grandiose and splendid or full of eccentricities carried to the extremes of fantasy. It was full of constant movement with swirling and broken rhythms. It was overdone with ornamentation or modified by classic restraint acquiring simplicity and stateliness. This phenomenon is evident in architecture, painting, sculpture, the decorative arts, landscape design and flower painting. Flower arrangement, as it has been known in the West, began during this period.

A remarkable book published in Rome in 1638, *Flora—ouero Cultura di Fiori*, by P. Giovanni Battista Ferrari of Sienna, shows the developing characteristics of the new style. Noted flower arrangers of the day composed flowers in vases to allow them to nod and sway on their stems. Here, too, is given the first printed account of the popular new fashion of drying flowers in sand. Ferrari's techniques will be given under "Sand-Drying" in Part Two.

The flower paintings of the Dutch and Flemish artists of the seventeenth and eighteenth centuries are masterpieces of baroque art. Exquisite portraits of favorite flowers appeared in exuberant masses of vibrant color. Masterly composition produced gorgeous decorative effects.

This distinctive and highly developed style of flower painting spread through Europe, and flower arrangement has been influenced by it to the present day.

The rococo style was the extreme development of the baroque, yet it was an original and distinctly French product of the Louis XV period. It is characterized by delicacy and the decorative use of asymmetrical arrangments of curves and countercurves. It was the high fashion throughout Europe in the first half of the eighteenth century but had little influence in England and America until the last half of the century.

The classic revival style was the outgrowth of interest in the study of ancient precedents of Rome and the exciting discoveries revealed in the excavations at Pompeii and Herculaneum. It came into vogue after the middle of the eighteenth century in England and France but did not reach America until after the Revolution.

The new style was greatly admired for its dignity and formality. It possessed classic symmetry. Straight lines and precise geometric curves were a welcome change from the exaggerated rhythms of the preceding styles. Flowers do not lend themselves to precise symmetry, but the containers in which they were arranged were of classic form.

The romantic era of the nineteenth century, often referred to as the

Victorian period, saw a search for a style to express its humanitarian ideals, its deep sentiment, and its belief in progress. It was thought that lessons learned from the past would provide a guide for the future. This enthusiasm brought a succession of revival styles. First, as has been seen, the Roman, then the Greek, rapidly followed by the Gothic, Medieval, Renaissance, Baroque and Rococo.

Inspiration for flower arrangement fashions and fads was sought from the eagerly awaited periodicals of the day. In them was presented a wealth of information to guide the busy fingers, minds and hearts of the ladies. Many contrived and sentimental floral decorations were high style.

The French tradition of flower painting was carried forward in this era. Invaluable lessons in color and patterned composition can be learned from these paintings.

Art Nouveau emerged as an original style at the end of the era. After the imitations of the past, it was a refreshing experience. There was emphasis on naturalism and good craftsmanship.

At the turn of the century, in the Edwardian period in England, elegance and sophistication replaced Victorian sentimentality.

The flower arrangement styles of the historical periods of Europe mentioned have greatly influenced contemporary styles, and the art of Japan has also played a most significant role.

A glimpse into the long history of Japanese flower arrangement indicates that Buddhist priests directed much of the development of the classic styles. The oldest school, *Ikenobo,* can be traced back to the sixth century when *Ono-no-Imoko,* who had studied in China, brought back the custom of floral offerings for Buddhist altars.

By the eleventh century a formal highly stylized temple art had evolved called *Rikkwa* or *Rikka.*

In the fifteenth century, Zen Buddhism and the Tea Ceremony exerted a vital influence on all aspects of flower arrangement with spontaneity, restraint and simplicity being emphasized in arranging flowers as a poetic expression.

During this period the classic style of the *Ikenobo* school called *Showka* or *Shoka* was developed, reached near perfection in the eighteenth century and is still in favor today.

New schools in the late eighteenth and early nineteenth centuries deviated from the *Shoka* style by employing exaggerated bending of branches and more than one kind of material. Two still in existence are the *Enshu-ryu* and *Ko-ryu.*

Nageire, an informal style, was practiced outside religious circles along with *Rikka.* Its popularity increased in the sixteenth century with the Tea Ceremony.

Flower arrangement assumed a position of such importance in Japanese life that large exhibitions were held as early as the sixteenth century, and this enthusiasm continues today.

The *Moribana* style, both informal and naturalistic, is a twentieth-century development. It shows some western influence and provides leeway for personal expression.

Variations of all the styles gained prominence in many schools with many teachers during the long history.

Contemporary Japanese styles have broken with tradition. One sees in exhibitions today many arrangements of free style that are dramatic and imaginative.

Some of the most noted schools teach both traditional and modern styles, and *Ikebana* has become international. Among the well-known schools are *Ohara, Sogetsu* and *Ichyo*.

The flower arrangement of East and West developed under conditions so separate that each remained until modern times unaffected by the other. In the Western World, flowers have been associated for the most part with man. They have appealed to his finer feelings and graced his life. In the development of the western mixed-bouquet art, one finds a welcome and enthusiastic acceptance of the beauty and bounty of nature and an enjoyment of a rich, full sense of color. Flower arrangements have been happily used for decoration of palace and cottage alike, and have played an important role in festivities and ceremonies.

In the East flowers have been thought of as a beautiful part of the great order of things in the universe, a part of nature of which man himself is a part. Flower arrangement has been approached from a contemplative, philosophic and poetic point of view. Flower masters and disciples alike sought to grasp the essential attributes of beauty of flowers in nature and attempted to portray through selection, symbolism and design not what was seen, but what was felt.

It is said that "art is a tryst" for in the joy of it, maker and beholder meet. In the East, art becomes a whole only when the beholder's imagination co-operates with the suggestion conveyed by the artist.

On the contemporary American scene, flower arrangements of all styles are in fashion, from the traditional styles of Europe, to the classical styles of Japan, to those of the latest concept in modern art—abstract.

Flower arrangement has reached a stage of great refinement through widening interest in its study and practice. Much credit is due the local, state and national garden clubs and Ikebana International.

Traditional design includes three main types—mass, line and massed-line. The mass reflects the European bouquet style, line types reflect the art of Japan, and the massed-line is an American development influenced by both East and West.

The most recent trend in contemporary styles is ever new-fashioned for it is developed to break with tradition and the familiar, following the tendencies in modern art.

Dried flowers and dried or treated foliage of distinctive quality have found a welcome place in contemporary design. The beautiful colors and exquisite natural forms achieved by good craftsmanship and methods, both new and old, make dried flowers appropriate and welcome material for flower arrangements of any style, traditional styles of historic periods as well as modernistic.

For the study of the history of flower arrangement, two books by American authors are invaluable. *Period Flower Arrangement*, by Margaret Fairbanks Marcus, and *A History of Flower Arrangement*, by Julia S. Berrall.

ITALIAN BAROQUE (1600–1700)   *Baroque*

The baroque style like the Renaissance had its beginning in Italy. The untrampled individualism and freedom from classic restraint is revealed in the irregular rhythmic movement and emotional fervor of the baroque.

It is fascinating to have a personal account of the enthusiasm felt for flower arrangement, gardens, floriculture, flower paintings, vases and baskets, pressed flowers, flower pictures, silk flowers and dried flowers— all found in the exceptional book by Ferrari that has already been mentioned.

Excerpts have been translated from the Italian to appear in this book. From them one can catch the feeling of excitement about the new fashions in flower arrangement and their use to decorate the homes of leading citizens in Rome. Many of the practices will be familiar for they are still in use today.

The chapter on flower arrangement is entitled, "Use and Marvels of Flowers," and begins, "Cultivation of flowers has one main objective: to gather them when in bloom and to organize them into beautiful indoor arrangements."

He describes the first type as the "usual bouquet" and admires Anastasio della Vetera, "a noble young man," who was skilled in preparing them. Hints and suggestions are given for anyone who might want to try the art. "Select flowers in season, fragrant, colorful, numerous. In the Rome region you will find an abundance of anemone, hyacinths, and narcissus in February and March," he writes. The detailed directions for assembling entails tying the flowers in a compact bouquet much like the tussy-mussy of Victorian days. These were made to be carried or to be placed in vases.

Next is noted "an arrangement of flowers to be used in winning the favor of Princes. Creator of this arrangement was Tranquillo Romauli, a man very famous for his magnificent garden." Custom-made wicker baskets were covered with myrtle, then several circles of flowers of different types and colors arranged close together according to size and color with a large outstanding flower placed in the center. He suggests that various patterns could be used according to "one's preference, taste, and imagination." He also mentions that other lovely types "are being constructed by Fabrizio Sbardoni and Giovanni Battista Martelletti, both men very famous for their ability of cultivating and arranging flowers." Flowers were also used in stylized forms. "Recently a beautiful ship was made of flowers and presented as a gift to Cardinal Carlo Pio." He laments the fact that these flowers lacked moisture and soon died, and compliments P. Horatius Grassi for devising new method vases of all shapes with intricate internal devices to hold water for short-stemmed flowers.

"If one prefers a simpler type vase," Ferrari continues, "here is one which I devised. I selected a clay vase because it reminded me of my own origin and because such material is suitable for a person who has little, and little is plenty for him. Rich people may use vases like mine, but made of gold and silver. . . . The cover of the vase is shaped like a cupola, with an opening at the top and many holes on the sides, in alternate rows, for the flowers. I have chosen such a cover because it can easily be removed, and the water can be easily poured out of the vase. This should be done every two or three days. The stems should be cut at the bottom as they decompose."

Then he gives directions in detail for mosaics made entirely of flowers. This type was introduced by Benedetto Drei, overseer of the furniture and fittings in the Vatican building. "This past year we have seen a flower mosaic representing the Prince of Apostles adoring Christ the Saviour, proclaiming His divinity and receiving the title of 'blessed'. The words were spelled out in letters for which bright flowers were used. The entire composition was so beautifully and realistically done that one could almost hear the words. Every year Rome has an opportunity to admire a magnificent work of this type in which flowers are transformed into divine heroes." First a drawing in color was made, then flowers were arranged according to the required color. "Thus, for example, for a human face carnations were used for the flesh and roses for the cheeks, which, with good reason, are called 'rosy'. A flower of dark blue color, almost black, was used for the pupils of the eyes. Such a flower could be the so-called *botryoid* hyacinth which grows in bunches along the road. The same

419

VAS OPERCVLO MVLTIFORO
AD FLORES ORDINATE CONTINENDOS

G*gg*-2

Figure 1. An illustration from Ferrari's book showing the vase he devised. "Flora,"
P. G. Battista Ferrari, The Pierpont Morgan Library.

dark flower can be used for the head and for the dark portions of the body. It can also be used for the hair, if dark. In the case of blond or white hair, the broom [*Genista*] and the white carnations can be used respectively. For the clothes is appropriate the blue flower known as 'Sperone di Cavaliere' [cone-shaped protuberance of the flower of dark-colored fig] or the bright red wild poppy or red carnations or also the golden brown and green myrtle. These flowers, so hard to find in the cities, are abundant in the country. The 'Sperone di Cavaliere' could be used for the air and the serene sky. Also suitable for these two items are the rose of Damascus and the jasmine."

So here is Ferrari's account of some of the flowers of the period. He also mentioned the tulip, which can be seen among the flowers in the vase he designed.

Other flowers seen in Renaissance paintings and those of this era also include:

Bachelor's Button	Lupine
Bellflower	Mallow
Buttercup	Marigold
Columbine	Monkshood
Daisy	Morning-glory
Forget-me-not	Narcissus (*N. Bulbocodium,*
Honeysuckle	*Jonquilla poeticus, Tazetta,*
Iris	*triandrus*)
Laurel or Sweet Bay	Pansy
Lemon	Pinks
Lily (*Lilium candidum, martagon,*	Primrose
umbellatum)	Stock
Lily-of-the-valley	Violet

In the chapter on "Secrets of Cultivation of Flowers," he writes, "I consider art wanting and unworthy of praise if it competes with nature and tries only to imitate but not surpass it. It is a justified complaint, which we hear everyday from everybody, that most gardeners are too busy acquiring new varieties of flowers and neglect to perfect the cultivation of those they already produce." He lists the wonders sought for flowers—to have them grow out of season, to obtain in them new shades of color, to change their odor from unpleasant to pleasant, to change, in many ways, their shape. Then he tells, "In our praiseworthy and daring undertaking we have the timely assistance of an informative lecture given recently during an academic assembly by Andrea Capranica, a Roman man very illustrious by both birth and knowledge. With this lecture he brings out the light of gardens from their deep hidden places, the secrets of chemical science." Advice on using chemicals, compost and blood of dead animals to stimulate growth is given, much as is done today.

The chapter, "Arbitrary Season of Flowers," deals with forcing. "What perfect virtue accomplishes in the souls of men, cultivation accomplishes in the garden so that, like man, a flower can be ready at any given time. Thus, either by anticipating bloom or by delaying it or by extending it, we can enjoy spring in any season and at our will." He refers to methods used in ancient Rome and quotes from Pliny.

Beautiful pottery was made in Italy during this period and glazes included midnight-blue, green, milk-white, purple or copper luster. Craftsmanship in metal work was superb. Vases were ornamented with gadrooning, embossed, engraved and enameled. Venetian glass was lovely in deep blue and purple, as well as clear crystal, or with enameled decoration in jewel colors.

The arrangement of the Italian baroque style in Color *Plate* 1* is presented in a two-tiered wicker basket, a popular container of the day. In the lower basket lies a classic stylized wreath of Cheerfulness daffodils and ivy. In the top basket, the flowers: tulips, hyacinths and daffodils, sway and nod on their stems in rhythmic movement characteristic of the new baroque style.

DUTCH-FLEMISH PERIOD (17th and 18th CENTURIES)

Freedom from Spanish rule and expansion of trade brought a new middle class to power in government and business which became the patrons and collectors of art and the enthusiastic developers of gardens.

Gardeners and floral connoisseurs were sheer fanatics in their culture and improvement of native varieties and new flowers brought home from around the world by seafaring merchants. The "Tulipmania" is but a single manifestation of the huge sums of money expended.

Collectors employed artists to portray each favorite and triumph; this was accomplished with exquisite perfection and fidelity to detail, even to the dewdrops, spiders and ants. These portraits were composed in hundreds of flower paintings of which many are masterpieces of baroque form.

Jan Brueghel (1568–1625) was the most prolific flower painter of the Flemish School. He collaborated more than once with Peter Paul Rubens, renowned for his splendid paintings in the baroque style. In Rubens' "The Madonna in a Garland of Flowers," Brueghel's garland is a riotous display of colorful flowers freely disposed and unrestricted by the rigid symmetry of the classic form.

---

* All plates to which I refer will be found following pages 50 or 130.

Figure 2. "Vase of Flowers," by Jan Davidsz de Heem (d. 1649). The whites of poppy, guelder rose and Queen Anne's lace are sharply contrasting with the rich reds, blues and soft greens. Poppies on their curving stems, and the Bybloem tulips shown in profile are both typically placed and give a feeling of depth. The usual butterflies hover about the flowers, and the expected snail and lizard appear at the base, but wheat and garden peas are not often seen. Reproduced through the courtesy of the National Gallery of Art, Andrew Mellon Fund.

Ambrosius Bosscharet's (1609–45) "Flowers on a Window Sill," in a jeweled glass, tumbler-shaped vase, is a symmetrical triangular design of soft, warm color harmony, a beautiful and distinctive work much appreciated by those who enjoy having baroque movement held within precise bounds. Paintings by Ottmar Elliger (1633–79) are similarly composed.

Willem van Aelst (1626–88) painted bold designs with arching lines in asymmetrical balance and vibrant color contrasts.

Jan Davidsz de Heem (1606–83/4), as an objective painter, advanced flower painting to a point far in advance of what had gone before, and his influence was unmistakable. His "Vase of Flowers," in Figure 2, demonstrates many of the characteristics of the Dutch-Flemish art of flower painting. Free-flowing lines, swirling rhythms, contrasting color schemes and dramatic shapes in a lively silhouette are typically employed. Flowers of all seasons in exuberant oval masses overpowered their containers and spilled over to lie at the base. The S-curve was sometimes used within the overall symmetry. The compositions acquired the appearance of being three-dimensional through the turning of heads to display their backs or show them in profile, and through the overlapping of flowers, some deeper in the arrangement than others. Each flower was accurately painted to reveal the artist's recognition of the beauty of its structure, and each appeared uncrowded in the full bouquet. Deeply cut, veined and curling forms of poppy and other foliage contributed to the baroque curves. Rose foliage exhibited greater textured interest from the back, and slender blades provided contrast.

Large flowers, conspicuous in the outline and borne on prominent curved stems, were favorites—red and white poppies with their drooping buds; the beloved tulip, particularly the Bizarres and Byblooms with their striped and flecked markings; lovely pink and white damask and cabbage roses, and the yellow sulphur rose; white and rose peonies; lavender, blue, yellow and white iris exhibiting their flaring, jaunty charm; orange turkscap and white Madonna lilies; and white and pink hollyhocks. These same flowers were spotted throughout the design or flowed over the rim of the container. Delphinium appeared late in the period.

The dramatically shaped crown imperial (*Fritillaria imperialis*), both red and orange, appeared frequently and was placed high either at the top or off-center.

Patterned shapes, somewhat smaller in size, played supporting and contrasting roles—anemone, both single and double, of red, white, pink, lavender and mauve; the white guelder rose or snowball (*Viburnum opulus sterile*); both African and French marigolds often outstanding with their contrasting orange color; carnations or clove gilliflower, white and pink variegated; the guinea-hen flower (*Fritillaria meleagris*) checkered, dark purple or lavender or sometimes yellow; orange calendula; daisies and primroses of many colors, particularly the *Primula auricula*.

Straight spike flowers were seldom featured, but elongated forms of such flowers as the Roman hyacinth, deep blue and white, curved gracefully instead. Sprays of fruit blossoms; yellow and white narcissus; pale blue forget-me-not; dainty lily-of-the-valley, yellow buttercups, clear blue morning-glories added further variety; and jasmine, blue and white columbine, honeysuckle, and small dainty flowers were swept to all points of the silhouette on their long, delicate and curving stems.

Butterflies fluttered about the flowers and snails, lizards, insects, shells and flowers completed the overflow at the base of the container.

Beautifully shaped containers of many kinds appeared. Heavy, handsomely decorated glass tumblers and jugs, clear glass goblets and flasks, metal urns shaped with swirling lines, and the lovely delft pieces the Dutch craftsmen made to take the place of the expensive Chinese blue-and-white porcelain.

Jan van Huysum (1682–1749), if not actually "The Prince of Flower-Painters," as he is styled in Colonel M. H. Grant's book "Jan van Huysum," has been recognized as a master. Jan and Jakob van Os, Paul Theodore van Brussel, the two van Spaëndoncks and Rachel Ruysch were accomplished painters.

Van Huysum had a perfect flair for composition. His studied color harmonies, and the contrasting of light flowers against dark created gorgeous effects. Balance-counterbalance areas of interest brought vital rhythms and a dynamic quality to his designs.

His exquisitely painted flowers and foliage with delightful textural quality were loosely disposed to provide nodding room in the characteristic oval form. The silhouette was not always closed. Great emphasis was given dramatic shapes in the outline through interesting spacing.

The swirling movement, sweeping lines of stems, the use of dainty, as well as large, flowers to enliven the outline—all these techniques used by earlier painters were wonderfully handled by van Huysum. He employed a greater use of accessories to complete his designs. Fruits, including grapes, apricots, apples, pears, plums; and flowers, vines and nuts; bird's nests with eggs, appeared in many of his paintings, as well as the familiar snails, lizards, butterflies, ants and spiders.

Terra-cotta containers embellished with cupids, classical figures and festooned with flowers, all in bas-relief, were his favorites. Some were round, full-footed urns, and others *cachepot* types. He sometimes used large, globular clear glass, and vases of yellow-brown or reddish clay and ochre or amber colored clay.

The arrangement in *Plate 2* was composed to catch "the spirit of" the flower paintings of this period. Flowers of all seasons were used as the artists had done. Because the arrangement was used as part of an educational exhibit, "The History of Flower Arrangement," at the National Capital Flower Show, Garden Club Section, in 1969, only "authentic" kinds of flowers known to have been grown during the period appear. Some, however, are a different variety because of hybridization. Rich, warm colors are typically contrasted by the pale colors of roses, hollyhocks, the guelder rose and carnations. The French and African marigolds are the familiar orange often found in the full bouquets. The lily, high off-center, repeats the orange color. Bybloem and Bizarre tulips with their striped markings are displayed characteristically in profile. Delphinium and hyacinth are the blue of the Dutch sky. Ranunculus and buttercups contribute to a lively outline. Peonies and peony foliage, favorites of van Huysum, were used, and red anemone lean over the lip of the red clay bowl. A butterfly is alight at bottom left in the design, and shells, pomegranates, a tulip and bird's nest rest at the base.

Louis XIV Period (1661–1715)

The most magnificent court in all Europe, established under Louis XIV, *Le Roi Soleil*, at Versailles, became the center of the cultural, social and political activity of France. Daily life, as well as ceremonial occasions, was regimented by strict rules of etiquette.

The baroque style was the vehicle employed by noted architects and artists to provide the sumptuous, luxurious and artistic setting that was Versailles. Charles Le Brun, a noted painter, was appointed director of the Gobelins, where not only the fabulous tapestries were made, but also every class of furniture and furnishings for the royal palace and national buildings.

One of the famous Gobelin tapestries depicting a reception given by the absolute Monarch for the Spanish Ambassador shows the use of flowers from the vast gardens and enormous *l'orangerie* to further enhance the elaborately decorated grand salon. One entire wall is lined with flower arrangements in large urns held high on tall pedestals.

Le Brun, himself, is known to have filled massive stone and marble urns with flowers to achieve notes of color in the parterres of the green gardens designed by Lenôtre.

Jean-Baptiste Monnoyer, a Flemish artist, was commissioned by Le Brun to provide flower designs for the Gobelin tapestries. He is noted for his

Figure 3. Engraving by Jean-Baptiste Monnoyer (1634–99), from *Le Livre de Toutes Sortes de Fleurs d'après Nature*. An unmistakable French feeling pervades this light, airy baroque design of sweeping curves. Reproduced through the courtesy of the Metropolitan Museum of Art, Rogers Fund.

exceptional portfolio of engravings, *Le Livre de Toutes Sortes de Fleurs d'après Nature*. Figure 3 is one example of the lightness, elegance and grace of the most finished decorative designs that he executed.

A flower painting by Monnoyer, "Flowers in a Gilded Urn," is somewhat similar in composition to those of the Dutch painter, Jan van Huysum, but is distinctly French because of the lighter, more subtle color harmony and the elimination of the exaggerated use of accessories.

The flower arrangements seen in the paintings of Blain de Fontenay (1653–1715) and A. F. Desportes (1661–1743) sprang from the Dutch-Flemish tradition, but had the light, graceful touch of French elegance and a harmonious combination of colors.

The most popular containers were massive, gilded urns elaborately decorated with allegorical figures, leaves, shells and gadroon.

The Gobelin tapestry, "Diana," representing "Earth" has a crimson ground enclosing a floral and architectural niche in rich and beautiful coloring, with a white background. On this ground is portrayed "Diana" worshiped by Cupid and flanked by flowers. Lovely garlands and bouquets, birds, squirrels, fountains, watering cans with perching birds, and garlands and cupids emblematically engaged in tending the earth and enjoying the flowers therefrom make an idyllic scene. The grace, delicacy and coloring mark the tapestry as truly French; however, Claude Audran's cartoon (c. 1700) does not exemplify the baroque style. Rather, one can see how characteristics of styles overlap. The slender proportions and some of the details are of classic design more in the Louis XVI classic revival style.

Besides the flowers noted for the previous periods, new kinds introduced were the lovely, small graceful species *Gladiolus*, snapdragon, and orange blossom from the three thousand orange trees grown in *l'orangerie*. In winter these trees were placed in silver tubs to decorate the Hall of Mirrors and other vast salons, and in summer used in the extensive formal gardens. André Michaux, the noted botanist, was sent by Louis XIV to America to collect new kinds of flowers for the gardens at Versailles.

The arrangement in *Plate* 3 was composed in "the manner of" the Louis XIV baroque style. Dried flowers in a large oval mass sweep in a diagonal direction. Not all the flowers used were of the period, but are appropriate in feeling and color. The container is a French baroque reproduction. Flowers used are tulips, roses, delphinium, peony, camellia, Dutch iris, globe thistle, carnations, statice, celosia, zinnia, lilac and hydrangea. Peony, annual poppy, Juliana barberry and cecropia foliage were also used.

Figure 4. Gobelin tapestry, "Diana," one of a series representing the four elements "Earth," "Water," "Fire," and "Air" portrayed by Diana, Neptune, Jupiter, and Juno. These cartoons by Claude Audran (c. 1700) include elements of the baroque and also classic elements of the Renaissance. Reproduced through the courtesy of the Corcoran Gallery of Art, Washington, D.C.

Early Georgian Period (1714–60)

The eighteenth century under the three Georges witnessed a brilliant flowering of all the arts. The growth of the colonial empire, the increase of trade and the acquisition of wealth prompted the building of splendid palaces and fine stately homes, and stimulated an elaborate social life.

The influence of the baroque style is seen in the architectural development and the sumptuous decorations and furnishings. It evolved as a restrained adaption of the continental style. Its relatively modest character can be explained in terms of the general restraint that characterized English taste in the arts, and by the fact that it had lost its impetus by the time it was introduced.

In architecture the popularity of the Italian classical style introduced by Inigo Jones (1573–1652) continued and modified the baroque style of the most noted architects of the period, the great Sir Christopher Wren, James Gibbs and Sir William Chambers, among others.

There was a passion for oriental porcelain (Queen Anne made a large collection of the blue and white) and other oriental arts, and houses were filled with treasures—tapestries, gilt and leather hangings, paintings, sculpture and other art objects, many of which were collected and brought back from trips to the continent, especially Venice and Rome. Educational trips were the fashion, and many students completed their educational studies by taking the "Grand Tour" through Europe. Edward Gibbon reported that in 1785 forty thousand English visitors were in Rome in a single season.

This was a great age of furniture design. At the turn of the century the William and Mary style was in force. It was of rectangular structure with baroque elements—scroll feet, curved arms, crested backs and scrolled turnings. Early in the century the Queen Anne style became popular. The most distinctive element that gave this style its simplicity and grace was the consistent use of the elongated S-curve.

By mid-century a more elegant and highly ornamental style developed finding its most handsome expression in the work of Thomas Chippendale. His unique gift for creating designs of great beauty enabled him to adapt the baroque style with influences of Gothic, Chinese and elements of the French rococo in a manner acceptable to the English taste.

The French rococo style gained favor about mid-century, and lighter colors and more delicate and fanciful decorative motifs were used.

It is significant that much of our knowledge of flower arrangements from this period is a direct result of the absorbing interest exhibited in horticulture and new plant introduction from America and other parts of the world. Plant explorers sent home plants from the New World for Queen Mary's collection at Hampton Court. Peter Collinson, Philip Miller and certain members of the aristocracy were responsible for the introduction into England of over one hundred and fifty new plants for their gardens. Peter Collinson's correspondence with John Bartram, the renowned American plant discoverer, lists many kinds.

The numbers of foreign plants coming into England, as well as the rest of Europe, made the production of books on "garden" plants a necessity. This was not the necessity of the original herbals, to guide those seeking medicines and balms, but rather the need for the beautiful.

Perhaps the most famous botanist in the world was Linnaeus. His greatest contribution was a system for naming and classifying plants giving each only two names, the first name for its genus and the second to designate its species. This eliminates confusion where the same plant will often have acquired a number of common names.

Drawing upon new ideas about nature, England developed a new style of landscape design. It consisted of a succession of "picturesque" land-scapes—a place to stroll about. The formal garden was passé. First laid out by Kent, this style was handled so well by Lancelot Brown that he acquired the name "Capability" Brown.

From writings we know that the English over a long period of history have loved gardening and used flowers and herbs to decorate and add fragrance to their rooms. There are, however, few flower arrangements seen in paintings, drawings or wall decorations. Landscapes were in vogue for backgrounds in the many portraits by Gainsborough, Romney, Reynolds and other noted artists of the day.

Robert Furber, a nurseryman at Kensington, published a series of prints, *Twelve Months of Flowers*, in 1730, that served as a catalogue from which seeds, plants and bulbs could be ordered. Peter Casteels, a Flemish artist, was commissioned to paint the series. The flowers appeared loosely and gracefully disposed, but being one of a kind serve best the purpose for which they were commissioned.

Jacob van Huysum, a Dutch painter, son of Justus and brother of the famous Jan, also painted a calendar series. These are composed more in the style of the flower paintings of the Dutch and Flemish, but definitely show the restraint more suited to English taste. The colors were not as flamboyant as those of the Dutch-Flemish and the rhythmic movement was subdued.

Small arrangements were used as a part of the mantel decor, as seen in the painting by William Hogarth, "The Lady's Last Stake." Boughpots filled with flowers were placed in the fireplaces in summer—a delightful custom sometimes followed today.

Flower arrangements showed the same qualities that characterized the arts and furnishings of the period. In general, they were of symmetrical balance, oval or pyramidical in form, and the height was two times or more or the same height as the container. Dark jewel colors were relieved with pale tones and white with striking green foliage. Flowers of velvety texture were popular and fragrance was greatly enjoyed.

Containers used by the two artists who painted the "Twelve Months of Flowers" series were generally sturdy, footed, wide-mouthed urns, sometimes interestingly decorated. Flower vases were manufactured in quantity by the busy ceramic factories at Bow, Chelsea, Worchester and Derby, to name but a few. Many were of fantastic shapes with applied decorations; some were handsomely painted reminiscent of those imported from China, and vases often had ingenious openings in the top to hold flowers in place.

In an article from the magazine *Antiques*—"Early Ceramic Flower Containers," by Nina Fletcher Little—this description is found:

> One English potter was especially interested in horticulture, and it is through his letters, and the products of his factory, that we are given a contemporary glimpse of the important role that flower arrangements played in eighteenth-century England. This man was Josiah Wedgwood, whose son John became the first treasurer of the Royal Horticultural Society of London, and one of whose daughters married Doctor Robert Darwin and became the mother of Charles Darwin, the great English naturalist. Wedgwood operated his pottery in Staffordshire from 1760 until his death in 1795, and during that time lavished a great deal of time and thought on his vases and root pots. He sought the advice of his customers and friends as to the styles which they preferred, and designed his pots accordingly. Some of his titled patrons, as he wrote to his partner Thomas Bentley, liked those containers with spouts, because "they say that sort keep the flowers distinct and clever." In the same letter, dated July 29, 1772, he wrote, "Vases are furniture for a chimney-piece, bough pots for a hearth, under a slab or marble table. I think they can never be used one instead of another." Of the materials which he used, creamware—perforated, festooned, or enameled—was one of the most popular. Cane color, black basalt with reliefs in red, and jasper in many different shades were used. We find such descriptions as "bouquetiers of red and white biscuit," "myrtle pans of cane-leaf pattern" "flower jars of purple and green enameled," and "bulbous root-pots in pebble and gold."

Some of the favorite flowers of the period, and there were many, were *Primula auricula* of twenty-six varieties; anemone, hyacinth, roses, tulips, iris, monkshood, carnation, feverfew, bellflowers, mignonette, delphinium, stock, lilies, and also many listed for the Dutch-Flemish period.

It is gratifying to find that dried flowers were used in this period. Philip Miller, author of *The Gardener's Dictionary*, wrote that the globe amaranth

Jacobus Van Huysum   IUNE:

(*Gomphrena globosa*) "are beautiful, and if gathered before they are too far advanced, retain their beauty for several years." Curtis's *Botanical Magazine*, in an early issue published late in this period, mentioned statice, or purple thrift—"The dried flowers are a pretty ornament for the mantelpiece in the winter."

The style of the arrangement in *Plate 4* was inspired by the calendar of arrangements by Jacob van Huysum. The Victorian container approximates the crater-shaped urns used in the paintings. The handsome peony and dogwood foliages which were dried in sand are a prominent feature of this composition. Elegant roses and tulips are important elements in the design. Transitional material is delphinium, lilac and double larkspur. Hydrangeas were used as the filler material. Contrasting flowers are pentstemon, deutzia, black-eyed Susans, *Viburnum carlcephalum*, Mexicana zinnias, columbine, love-in-a-mist, and verbena which suggests the auricula that was so much favored in eighteenth-century England.

Figure 5. Jacob van Huysum's composition for June from the book *Twelve Months of Flowers*, by Colonel M. H. Grant. Published by F. Lewis Ltd., Leigh on Sea, England. The description from the book reads:

"The month for happy marriages according to the Romans; The Summer *Zomer-Maand* to the Dutch; the *Joy Month* to our own ancestors, the Saxons. Two blooms of sacred allusion are prominent here, the *Passion Flower*, every part of which has a holy meaning; the *Pomegranate*, so revered by the Jews as to their embroidering it on the robes of their High Priest. The evil *Aconite* (*Monks Hood* or *Wolfsbane*) appears again in all its poisonous beauty, together with *Turk's Head Lilies*, *Canna*, several species of *Roses* and *Carnations*. The landscape in this piece is particularly pretty with its delicately brushed-in foliage and an airy distance relieved by a Gothic abbey, an unusual feature in these paintings. A Peacock and Painted Lady butterflies vie in colour with the lovely tints of the blooms above them. The Vase, with its classical relievo is a masterpiece of the kind of marvel whose High Priests were Jacob De Witt in Holland and Theodore De Bruyn imported thence into England. As an example of general *tone*, this is one of the finest of the series, and how difficult it is to preserve that almost indefinable attribute in so polychromatic a work as a flower-picture can be realised by other than painters."

EARLY AMERICAN (1607–99)

Colonial America was not one culture. The southern colonies, the New England colonies and the Dutch were settled by people of different backgrounds, culture and ambitions. Each developed its own characteristics in the hostile new land; as soon as the barest foothold was gained, attempts were made to recreate familiar patterns of living. Colonists built their houses and public buildings, made furniture and household utensils, planted gardens and painted pictures much like those they had left behind. However, the baroque style does not pertain to this period.

The colonies of Virginia, Maryland and the Carolinas reflected the aristocratic ideals and aspirations of England. Soon an agricultural empire was made up of large plantations along the waterways that connected them with each other and the mother country. By contrast, the New England colonies were settled by dissenters from the Church of England and their small towns and villages grew as adaptations of those they knew in southeastern England. New Amsterdam by the middle of the century was in many ways a replica of the city in Holland from which it took its name.

VIRGINIA COLONY

By the year 1615 Jamestown boasted two rows of houses of framed timber, with a small garden by each, and three substantial storehouses. Brick makers were among the first settlers of Jamestown, so it is not surprising to find that the house at Green Spring was built of brick by Sir William Berkeley after his arrival in Virginia to take up his duties as Royal Governor in 1642. He developed his estate according to ambitious plans, planting mulberry trees, 1500 fruit trees, laid out extensive rose gardens, and built a greenhouse for his orange trees. Bacon's Castle (1650–76) is patterned after the manor houses of the English gentry and still stands in Surrey County.

The commodious houses built in Virginia and Maryland before the end of the seventeenth century appear aristocratically grand in comparison with the New England structures of the same period. Because plantations were distant from each other, there was visiting back and forth between the families to dispel the loneliness, and the tradition of southern hospitality was begun.

Nothing is known as to how cut flowers were used during this period. It could be expected that Lady Berkeley would have had boughpots filled perhaps with dogwood, holly or bayberry placed in the fireplace during the summer, as was done back home in England. In anticipation of the arrival of guests, bouquets could have been made, perhaps of roses from the garden and a few orange blossoms for fragrance, in containers brought from England. Casual bouquets of flowers may have been placed in household jars or bowls to decorate the simple cottages of the small landowners and craftsmen.

There was early interest in the plant discoveries of the New World. The colonists at Jamestown sent home the red lobelia in 1629. Lord Burleigh sent John Tradescant in 1657 to collect plants for his fine garden at Hatfield, and he was the first to discover the Virginia creeper, the coneflower, columbine, lupine, aster, phlox, beebalm or bergamot. Also, according to his book Bishop Compton of London sent John Banister to Virginia in the dual role of priest and plant collector, and in 1678 he published *John Banister's Catalogue*, the first known catalogue of Virginia plants. France sent André Michaux, botanist to Louis XIV, one of the most important collectors, who paid his debt to the southern states by introducing the pink-flowering Albizzia, commonly called mimosa, the Chinaberry, the tea plant and the camellia. Familiar plants of England were also brought to Virginia. Joan Parry Dutton, in her delightful book *Enjoying America's Gardens*, reminds us that tradition says the women of Jamestown brought the daffodil with them in their aprons.

NEW ENGLAND

In New England the heavy timber-framed, clapboard-sheathed mode of construction characteristic of the last half of the seventeenth century left a permanent imprint on house design and construction in America. A number of these remarkable houses, some of the classic salt-box type, have been restored by historical societies and other organizations.

The interiors displayed the same vigor and honesty as the exteriors. The low-ceiling rooms are dominated by the structural timbers overhead and by the large fireplaces of stone or brick. The fine craftsmanship is noteworthy. The beautifully laid floor planks, the dark beams against smooth white plaster, the sturdy well-made furniture with straight lines and vigorous turnings characterized the well-ordered life of New England.

In these charming rooms a casual bunch of wildflowers, perhaps with some herbs tucked in, placed in a pottery bowl or pewter cup, would create just the right note of cheer to the modern eye. The lovely wildflowers that grew in New England included goldenrod, asters and black-eyed Susans, which may have been used alone or combined with those growing in the door-yard gardens, similar to those the settlers knew in England. Marigolds, roses, peonies, hollyhocks, coriander and rosemary were grown and used primarily for medicinal purposes and as seasoning.

John Josselyn made two trips to the colony, in 1638 and 1663, and wrote a book, *New England Rarieties Discovered*, in which he mentioned that gardens flourished with flowers, including those listed above, common to English gardens, and also that by his second trip fruit trees—apple, pear, quince, cherry and plum—had been introduced.

In *Plate 5* a cheerful bouquet, mostly field flowers, is composed in a stoneware jar. Goldenrod, scarlet sage, black-eyed Susans, Michaelmas daisies, rudbeckia, Queen Anne's lace, and pressed foliage of the sour gum tree were used.

DUTCH COLONY

In New Amsterdam, the use of colorful tiles and glazed bricks in pinks, yellows, oranges and dark purples, blues and blacks, was commented on by travelers who also noted the light, brightly painted interiors. These cheerful rooms were further enlivened by ceramics and pictures from Holland. Surely bouquets of favorite flowers were arranged in delft vases much as was done in Holland.

The Dutch brought their bulbs and love of flowers with them. Adriaen Van der Donck, in his *Description of the New Netherlands* (1655), mentions different kinds of tulips, anemones, lilies, gilliflowers and fritillaria, as well as roses. Several years later he found a variety of fruit trees growing in orchards.

COLONIAL GEORGIAN PERIOD (1700–76)

By the time of the Revolution, this country was well on its way toward competing with Europe in the elegance of its way of life and its arts.

During the eighteenth century rapid growth took place; people increasingly immigrated from all parts of Europe seeking an opportunity for a better life. The large number of slaves made possible the production of the big "money crop"—tobacco—and other agricultural products, and extended manufacture and trade contributed to the wealth and culture. The most tangible evidence of this remarkable economic and cultural growth is the imposing dignity and simple elegance of the Colonial Georgian mansions built by the mercantile princes of the North and the large plantation owners of the South.

The political dominance of England caused English cultural patterns to be all-pervasive at an early date. England set the standard in architecture, home furnishings, literature, art and dress. Even Benjamin Franklin, with his genuine belief in the validity of colonial life, advised his wife to follow the latest London fashions in home furnishing and decoration.

The colonial builders were influenced by the excellent work of Sir

Christopher Wren and by the books on design of other noted architects of England—Gibbs, William Salmon, Campbell, William Adam, Batty Langley, and others. These publications gave rules of proportion, design of details with sample plans, including interior design. The influence of these books was widespread from Portsmouth to Charleston.

The architecture and furnishings of the period are highlights in the history of American art and make it the most popular revival style. Houses

Figure 6. A blue and white arrangement reflecting Queen Mary's preference for Chinese porcelain in these colors. The delphinium, of various shades of blue, repeat the colors of the vase (a Williamsburg delft reproduction). White flowers are larkspur, Shasta daisies and acroclinium. The graceful green Christmas fern contributes a fresh look.

Figure 7. Catharine Hendrickson (painted 1770). American. Artist unknown. The arrangement of carnations is rather stiff, seemingly a characteristic of the artist's style. It is unusual indeed to find a bouquet in addition to a charming landscape in portraiture of the period. The flowers, the robin's red breast, the cardinal and the lady's gown are all rust-red. Reproduced through the courtesy of the National Gallery of Art, Washington, D.C., The Garbisch Collection.

of historical significance have been authentically restored and furnished by many different organizations and opened to the public. Others have been restored and adapted for modern living. Antique furniture and furnishings are collected and cherished. Reproductions and adaptations from architecture to craft items are everywhere and vary in quality from excellent to abominable.

Since there is almost no information available on flower arrangement, a look at historical settings, Colonial Williamsburg, Gunston Hall and the gardens at Mount Vernon, seems a good approach. The fine homes often filled with guests were the scene of lavish entertainment. The good taste exhibited in the decorations and furnishings certainly would have carried over into the creation of beautiful flower arrangements, which must have added to the feeling of hospitality.

Williamsburg, the capital of Virginia from 1699 to 1780, has been restored with scrupulous care for authenticity to make it the most vivid museum of the Colonial Georgian period. The principal appeal lies in its history and heritage, architecture, furniture and furnishings, gardens and handicrafts.

The luxurious elegance of the Governor's Palace is contrasted with the simple elegance of the town houses of the plantation owners, the fine homes of the professional men, and even more so, with the plain charm of the taverns, shops and homes of the tradespeople. The decoration and furnishings of the Palace span the period showing the evolution of popular styles of the day throughout the colonies in the more pretentious mansions. The walls were paneled with natural wood, waxed to a gleaming finish or painted in rich, mellow colors of bluish-green, stone-gray, tannish-buff, gray-blue, dull green and gold. In some rooms paneling was limited to the fireplace area, door and window trim, cornice (generally dentil), and the dado, all painted in the same mellow color as the plastered wall. Some walls were hung with handsome gilt leather hangings and also Chinese wallpaper, the latest fashion after mid-century.

The finer homes of the town were elegant but not ostentatious. The rooms were large and well-proportioned, with walls plastered and white-washed, or sometimes covered with wallpaper. Paneling was confined to the fireplace area, the door and window trim and dado, or even to a chair rail, molded cornice and baseboard, and was painted in the same or related warm, deep, muted colors as those seen in the Palace. Some marbelizing was also done.

The more modest homes, shops and taverns were clapboard structures with second-story dormer windows painted and contrastingly trimmed with the familiar mellow hues of stone, wood, and Spanish brown—a deep dull red. The interiors were finished in a fashion similar to the finer homes but simpler.

Most of the fine furniture and furnishings for the home of the Royal Governors were imported from England throughout the period. Furniture styles range from the early William and Mary, Queen Anne, and all the Chippendale variations, including the rococo. Rich, elegant fabrics of silk damask and lampas, cut velvets and crewel work were used for window and bed hangings, and needlework, brocades, damask, and leather covered the furniture. Crystal, brass and silver chandeliers and sconces were hung; Persian carpets, portraits, prints and mirrors contributed to the richness of the decor. The best English silver, pewter, china and glass, and also Chinese export porcelain, made up the lavish table appointments. A harpsichord stands in the ballroom where concerts are still held.

Certain homes, both the elegant and more modest, are furnished to reflect the known tastes and life style of the most noted owner during the period. Although much of the furniture and furnishings was imported from England, and orders for the latest fashions were often personally selected by the plantation owner's agent in London, skilled craftsmen were brought to the colonies to make furniture and other household goods, including silver. Books on furniture design were available, which included those by the master designer, Thomas Chippendale. The Windsor chair enjoyed a great popularity.

Fabrics from England were India chintz or calico, bold prints in rich colors of great variety, toile, stripes, plaids, damask and moreen, but home-spun linen and linsey-woolsey were made locally. Needlework was an art form as well as a pastime for the ladies who worked in needlepoint, crewel, quilting, turkey-work, samplers and other embroidery. For the more modest homes, simple furniture, as well as the Windsor chair, was made locally.

Potters attempted only to supply everyday household articles made from native clay. Glazed earthenware, called slipware, was decorated with scratch designs, dots, marbleized, or combed. Stoneware was salt-glazed and often decorated with cobalt-blue designs. The finer table wares were brought from England—Chelsea, Derby, Bow, Bristol, Worchester, Rockingham, Staffordshire, Wedgwood, Oriental Lowestoft and others. All manner of containers for flowers were imported—flower horns or wall pockets, containers with removable perforated lids, and bricks with perforated tops to hold flowers in place, boughpots, and vases of many shapes.

Louise B. Fisher, in her book, *An Eighteenth-Century Garland*, tells of her careful study and experience in regard to both fresh and dried flower arrangements made to decorate the rooms of the Governor's

Palace and exhibition homes in Colonial Williamsburg. Her work established a style in the eighteenth-century tradition.

The town boasts a silversmith, printing office, bookbinder, gunsmith, a forge, cabinetmaker, barber and peruke maker, apothecary shop, a spinning and weaving house where linsey-woolsey, homespun linen and other fabrics were loomed, a boot and shoemaker, and millinery shop. One can step into the historic past, watch craftsmen and journeymen at work with the tools used in the eighteenth century, walk in the gardens, eat and drink in the taverns and inns of yesteryear, hear the music, enjoy the drama, and many other eighteenth-century activities carried on in this wonderfully restored colonial capital.

Gunston Hall is a splendid example of the many beautiful plantation houses of Virginia. It is located in Fairfax County, and most notable because of its builder and owner, its decorator, and its gardens.

Gunston Hall was the home of George Mason, author of Virginia's Declaration of Rights, from which the Bill of Rights of the American Constitution was written, a pioneer of the Virginia Constitution, and one of the framers of the Constitution of the United States. The house which overlooks the Potomac was built between 1753 and 1758. William Buckland, when an indentured servant, designed and was responsible for the ornate and exquisitely carved woodwork. He created rooms of outstanding richness and beauty, with door and window trim unparalleled in elaboration in Virginia. These he derived or adapted from the great style books of the period, particularly the book by William Salmon, *Palladio Londinensia*. The Chinese Chippendale room, in the latest fashion brought by Buckland from London, is the only one of its kind in Virginia, and the Palladian room is perhaps the most important example of carved decoration of its period in America. It is so described by Thomas Tileston Waterman in his book, *The Mansions of Virginia*.

This mansion with its grounds was willed to the State of Virginia in 1945 by Mr. Louis Hertle, the last owner, who directed that the Colonial Dames of America should be the custodian. This organization has accomplished the furnishing of the Hall with wonderfully crafted pieces of that era, a few of which were originally in the house.

George Mason laid out the gardens and planted the now majestic boxwood that are their main feature. The Restoration Committee of The Garden Club of Virginia was responsible for restoring this mid-eighteenth-century garden and presented it in April 1954. The Hall and gardens are open to the public.

The Palladian drawing room inspired the creation of the flower arrangement in *Plate 6*, which becomes an integral part of the entire room. The placement on the Adam mantel dictated the arrangement's size and shape.

Figure 8. The Palladian drawing room, Gunston Hall, derives its name from the designs of Andrea Palladio adapted by William Buckland for the elaborate carvings. The family and guests played games and had evening tea here.

The container chosen is an antique Chinese export porcelain brick with Chinese figures. Red is the dominant color in the arrangement just as red is the dominant color in the room, since three walls are covered with scarlet silk brocade. Roses and tulips were chosen not only for their shades of red, but also because of their refined textural quality. Red celosia, both crested and prince's feather, provide additional reds and also contrast in form and texture. Red button zinnias and strawflowers, being small round forms, add interest, and the green Christmas fern fronds add an element of freshness.

The portrait of George Mason's wife, Ann Eilbeck, painted by Boudet suggested the other colors used. Larkspur and love-in-a-mist reflect the blue of her gown, while the flush on her cheeks is captured by the pinks of larkspur and strawflowers. Feverfew, the tiny daisy-like flowers, add sparkle and liveliness.

The broad hall leading from the "land" to the "river" door, cooled by the breezes from both directions, was used as a living room in the summer. Dances were held here and the Virginia "hunt board," on which the arrangement in *Plate* 7 stands, was used for serving stand-up meals for guests just in from hunting. The large oval form of this arrangement overpowers the sturdy apothecary jar, a Williamsburg delft reproduction. The rhythmic movement is carried by the use of the large red cockscomb placed off-center at the top and down through the arrangement to form the lazy-S so characteristic of the baroque style. Flower heads are turned to give a feeling of depth. The outline is lightened through the use of peony foliage and the sprightly foliage of the trumpet vine.

Visitors to this historic house during the summer months enjoy the fresh flowers from the garden which are arranged and placed in several rooms by members of the Officers' Wives Garden Club, Fort Belvoir, Virginia, and the Hallowing Point Garden Club of Lorton, Virginia. During the winter months dried arrangements are used to decorate the rooms. These bouquets give a warm, lived-in feeling, and visitors enjoy flowers—both fresh and dried—used "in the manner of" the style of George Mason's day. Amazement is often expressed that the dried flowers are so colorful. The question often asked is, "are these real flowers?" Only flowers known to have been grown in the gardens in Virginia in the mid-eighteenth century and native wild flowers are used in this historic house. The methods used in their preservation were those known at that time —air-drying, sand-drying and pressing.

When making arrangements for rooms of the Colonial Georgian period it is helpful to follow the advice of Margaret Fairbanks Marcus in her book, *Period Flower Arrangement,* "Too often we are tempted to make compositions so consciously styled that our conception of eighteenth century forms cannot be mistaken. But there are English, French, and American variants of the eighteenth century spirit. Too elegant an arrangement may well look French, one too heavily loaded may be mistaken for English Georgian. A happy medium can be found."

Great pleasure was taken in the development of gardens. The plantation owners located their homes to provide wide vistas, often overlooking the rivers that were their connecting link. After mid-century, formality gave way to informality and naturalistic landscaping to follow the new style in England.

Many old Virginia gardens have been restored as nearly as possible to their original eighteenth-century appearance in which only the plants known in that period are grown. Among the most notable are the gardens at Colonial Williamsburg, Mount Vernon, Gunston Hall, Monticello (the home of Thomas Jefferson) and the University of Virginia gardens which Jefferson designed.

Figure 9. A red, white and blue arrangement in Chinese porcelain in its setting, the Virginia Room, Memorial Continental Hall, DAR, Washington, D.C.

This was a great era of plant exploration and plant exchange between the colonies and England, encouraged and fostered by Peter Collinson of London who was passionately devoted to horticulture. From his correspondence with John Bartram of Pennsylvania and John Custis of Williamsburg detailed information is available.

John Bartram was self-taught and called by Linnaeus, the greatest natural botanist in the world. He introduced to cultivation more than 150 new species, and to his botanical garden on the Schuylkill River came plants from Europe.

John Custis was the largest importer of European plants in this period. He worked to expand the list in his garden which were hardy, and in his words, "Virginia proof."

John Clayton, Clerk of Gloucester County, Virginia, collected plants for the surrounding Tidewater area for his garden. He was largely responsible for the first complete botanical manual of the New World, *Flora Virginica.*

Mark Catesby of England, a poetic naturalist who helped John Custis and John Clayton with their gardens, wrote and illustrated *The Natural History of Carolina, Florida and the Bahama Islands,* an outstanding work which influenced the career of John James Audubon.

The landscape plan at Mount Vernon, Virginia, the home of George Washington, is a blend of the formal and informal styles of the eighteenth century. It was derived from designs by celebrated European landscape architects of the period, with variations in dimension, scale, and plant material adapted to the local situation. The principal features that George Washington eventually selected for his ornamental landscape or "pleasure grounds" included a Courtyard, the Bowling Green, Shrubberies, Groves, Wildernesses, Serpentine Avenues and beyond a Ha! Ha! Wall. A greenhouse, or "Orangerie," was constructed and parterres were planted in a fleur-de-lis motif. Two formal gardens were laid out: the Kitchen Garden in 1760 and the Flower Garden several years later.

Under the Mount Vernon Ladies' Association of the Union, restoration of the gardens has been accomplished with care for authenticity from plans and other detailed information available. All the ornamental herbaceous plant materials grown in the Flower Garden today are noted in the garden publications, correspondence, catalogues and lists of American gardeners of the eighteenth century.

The Flower Garden Planting List is reproduced through the courtesy of the Mount Vernon Ladies' Association of the Union. Since George Washington actively acquired new plants for his garden until the time of his death in 1799, this list would be correct for the Federal period.

MOUNT VERNON GARDENS

The Flower Garden Planting List

KEY:

  a) Annuals
  b) Biennials
  g) Potted and tubbed greenhouse plants
  p) Perennials
  s) Shrubs
  *) Plants mentioned in the Mount Vernon domestic records.
     Numerals indicate period of bloom in months

Aaron's-rod	*Thermopsis caroliniana*	p, 7–9
African daisy, or yellow ageratum	*Lonas annua*	a, 6–9
African marigold	*Tagetes erecta*	a, 8–10
Aloe, or century plant	*Agave americana*	g.
Alpine wall-cress, or rock-cress	*Arabis alpina*	p, 4–5
American cowslip, or shooting star	*Dodecatheon Meadia*	p, 4
Angel's-trumpet	*Datura arborea*	g, 1–4
Annual poinsettia	*Euphorbia heterophylla*	a, 7–9
Ascending, or blue lobelia	*Lobelia syphilitica*	p, 5–6
Atamasco lily	*Zephyranthes Atamasco*	p, 4
Austrian rose	*Rosa foetida*	s, 5–6
Autumn daffodil	*Sternbergia lutea*	p, 9
*Bachelor's button, or globe amaranth	*Gomphrena globosa*	a, 6–10

*Banana, West Indian plantain, or Adam's apple	*Musa paradisiaca*	g, 11
Bear's-breeches	*Acanthus mollis*	g.
Belladonna lily	*Amaryllis Belladonna*	g, 8
Black-eyed susan	*Rudbeckia hirta*	p, 7–9
Blazing star	*Liatris spicata*	p, 6–7
Blue lily, or lily-of-the-Nile	*Agapanthus orientalis*	g, 6–7
Blue perennial flax	*Linum perenne*	p, 5–9
Blue sophora, or false indigo	*Baptisia australis*	p, 5
Boneset, or thoroughwort	*Eupatorium perfoliatum*	p, 7
Bouncing Bet, or sopewort	*Saponaria officinalis*	p, 7–9
Bugle-weed	*Ajuga reptans*	p, 6
Butterfly-weed or New England dogbane	*Asclepias tuberosa*	p, 6–9

Cabbage rose	*Rosa centifolia*	s, 5–6
Canada bloodwort, or bloodroot	*Sanguinaria canadensis*	p, 4
Canadian columbine	*Aquilegia canadensis*	p, 4–6
Canterbury bells	*Campanula Medium*	p, 5–7
Cape aster	*Aster capensis*	g, 1–10
*Cardinal flower	*Lobelia cardinalis*	p, 6–8
Carnation, or clove pink	*Dianthus Caryophyllus*	g, 1–6
Castor bean, or palma christi	*Ricinus communis*	a, 7–10
China aster	*Callistephus chinensis*	a, 8–9
China, or Indian pink	*Dianthus chinensis*	a, 6–9
China, or monthly rose	*Rosa chinensis semperflorens*	s, 5–11
*China-rose hibiscus	*Hibiscus Rosa-sinensis*	g, 2–10
Chinese day-lily, or plantain-lily	*Hosta ventricosa*	p, 6–8
Christmas rose	*Helleborus niger*	p, 1–4
Clary	*Salvia Sclarea*	a, 7–9
Cockscomb	*Celosia cristata*	a, 8–10
*Coffee tree	*Coffea arabica*	g.
Common adder's-tongue	*Erythronium americanum*	p, 4
Common annual candytuft	*Iberis amara*	a, 5–7
Common foxglove	*Digitalis purpurea*	b, 6
Common laurustinus	*Viburnum Tinus*	g.
Common marvel of Peru, or four-o'clock	*Mirabilis Jalapa*	a, 7–9
Common passion flower	*Passiflora caerulea*	g, 2–9

Common periwinkle	*Vinca minor*	p, 5
Common sea lavender	*Limonium vulgare*	p, 8–9
Common stock	*Matthiola incana*	a, 5–10
Common thrift, or sea pink	*Armeria maritima*	b, 5–6
Cornflower, or blue-bottle	*Centaurea Cyanus*	a, 6–10
Corn marigold, or yellow boy	*Chrysanthemum segetum*	a, 6–9
Cow herb	*Saponaria Vaccaria*	b, 5–6
Cowslip	*Primula veris*	p, 4–6
*Crape myrtle	*Lagerstroemia indica*	s, 8–9
Crimson monarda, or bergamot	*Monarda fistulosa*	p, 7–9
Crocus rose, or globeflower	*Kerria japonica flore-pleno*	s, 5–8
Crown daisy	*Chrysanthemum coronarium*	a, 6–9
*Crown imperial	*Frittillaria imperialis*	p, 4
Cudweed	*Helichrysum petiolatum*	g.
Cup-and-saucer	*Campanula Medium calycanthema*	b, 5–7
Cupid's-dart	*Catananche caerulea*	p, 6–9
Daffodil, or Lent lily	*Narcissus Pseudo-Narcissus*	p, 4–5
Damask rose	*Rosa damescena*	s, 5–6
Double creeping buttercup	*Ranunculus repens flore-pleno*	p, 5–6
Double dwarf almond	*Prunus glandulosa flore-pleno*	s, 4–5
Dutch iris, or Spanish flag	*Iris Xiphium*	p, 4–5
Dwarf iris	*Iris pumila*	p, 4
Eastern, or oriental poppy	*Papaver orientale*	p, 4–5
English daisy	*Bellis perennis*	b, 5–7
English iris, or Pyrenean flag	*Iris xiphioides*	p. 6
English ivy	*Hedera Helix*	p.
*English, or Dutch boxwood	*Buxus sempervirens suffruticosa*	s.
English, or horned violet	*Viola cornuta*	b, 3–7
Evergreen, or globe	*Iberis sempervirens*	p, 4–5
*Everlasting pea candytuft	*Lathyrus undulatus*	p, 5–8
False chamomile	*Boltonia asteroides*	p, 8–9
Fern-leaved meadowrue	*Thalictrum minus adiantifolium*	p, 6–7
Fine-leaved peony	*Paeonia tenuifolia*	p, 5
Floss flower	*Ageratum Houstonianum*	a, 6–10

Flowering tobacco	*Nicotiana affinis*	a, 7–9
Forget-me-not	*Myosotis alpestris*	b, 5–7
French marigold	*Tagetes patula*	a, 8–10
French rose	*Rosa gallica*	s, 5–6
Garden balsam	*Impatiens Balsamina*	a, 6–8
Garden heliotrope, common valerian, or all heal	*Valeriana officinalis*	b, 6–8
Garden hyacinth	*Hyacinthus orientalis*	p, 4
Garden, or sweet rocket	*Hesperis matronalis*	p, 5–7
*Geranium, or horseshoe geranium	*Pelargonium zonale*	g, 3–9
German flag	*Iris germanica*	p, 5
Giant spider flower	*Cleome gigantea*	a, 6–10
Giant summer hyacinth	*Galtonia candicans*	a, 7
Gibraltar candytuft	*Iberis gibraltica*	a, 5–7
Globe flower	*Trollius europaeus*	p, 5
Globe thistle	*Echinops Ritro*	p, 7–10
Globe marguerite	*Anthemis tinctoria*	p, 6
Goldenrod	*Solidago canadensis*	p, 8
Grape hyacinth	*Muscari botryoides*	p, 4–5
Greater blue-bottle, or basket flower	*Centaurea montana*	p, 6
Great-flowered bell-flower	*Platycodon grandiflorus*	p, 6–8
Great honeywort	*Cerinthe major*	a, 6
Greek valerian	*Polemonium reptans*	p, 5
Guernsey lily	*Nerine sarniensis*	g, 7
Harison's yellow rose	*Rosa foetida Harisonii*	s, 5
Heliotrope, or Peruvian turnsole	*Heliotropium peruvianum*	g, 2–10
Hollyhock	*Althea rosea*	b, 6–7
Honesty	*Lunaria annua*	b, 5
Indian reed	*Canna indica*	a, 7–9
Ivy-leaved geranium	*Pelargonium peltatum*	g, 3–9
Jacob's ladder	*Polemonium caeruleum*	p, 6–7
Jamestown-weed, or jimson-weed	*Datura Stramonium*	a, 7–9
Jasmine, or jessamine	*Jasminum officinale*	g, 3–6
Jerusalem cherry	*Solanum Pseudo-Capsicum*	g, 11–12
Jonquil	*Narcissus Jonquilla*	p, 4–5
Joseph's-coat	*Amaranthus gangeticus melancholicus*	a, 7–10

King orange	*Citrus nobilis*	g, 3, 6
Large snapdragon	*Antirrhinum majus*	b, 5–10
*Larkspur	*Delphinium Ajacis*	a, 6
*Lemon	*Citrus Limonia*	g, 3, 6
Lily-of-the-valley	*Convallaria majalis*	p, 5
*Lime	*Citrus aurantifolia*	g, 3, 6
Long-tubed catmint	*Nepeta Mussini*	p, 5
Love-lies-bleeding, or flower gentle	*Amaranthus caudatus*	a, 7–10
Madagascar periwinkle	*Vinca rosea*	a, 7–10
Mandarin orange	*Citrus nobilis deliciosa*	g, 3, 6
Many-flowered zinnia	*Zinnia multiflora*	a, 8–10
Meadowrue	*Thalictrum speciosum*	p, 6–7
Meadow saffron, or autumn crocus	*Colchicum autumnale*	p, 9
Mist-flower	*Eupatorium coelestinum*	p, 7
Moon daisy	*Chrysanthemum maximum*	p, 6
Moss rose	*Rosa centifolia muscosa*	s, 5–6
Musk rose	*Rosa moschata*	s, 5–10
*Myrtle	*Myrtus communis*	g, 5
Nasturtium, or greater Indian-cress	*Tropaeolum majus*	a, 5–10
Nasturtium, or small Indian-cress	*Tropaeolum minus*	a, 5–10
New England aster	*Aster novae-angliae*	p, 8–9
Oak-leaved hydrangea	*Hydrangea quercifolia*	s, 6
*Oleander	*Nerium Oleander*	g, 5–9
*Opopanax	*Acacia Farnesiana*	g, 2–6
Ovate-leaved phlox, or lychnidea	*Phlox ovata*	p, 5
Pansy, or heartsease	*Viola tricolor*	b, 3–7
Paris daisy, or marguerite	*Chrysanthemum frutescens*	g, 3–9
Peach-leaved bellflower	*Campanula persicifolia*	p, 5–7
Penny-royal crane's-bill	*Pelargonium tomentosum*	g.
Peony	*Paeonia officinalis*	p, 6
Persian cyclamen, or sowbread	*Cyclamen persicum*	g, 2–5
Polyanthus	*Primula Polyantha*	p, 4–6
*Pomegranate	*Punica Granatum*	g.

Poppy anemone	*Anemone coronaria*	p, 3–5
Pot marigold	*Calendula officinalis*	a, 5–10
Prickly lantana	*Lantana Camara*	g, 2–10
Primrose	*Primula vulgaris*	p, 5–7
Prince's-feather	*Celosia cristata pyramidalis*	a, 8–10
Prostrate gypsophila	*Gypsophila repens*	p, 5
Purple-cup't statice	*Limonium sinuatum*	b, 6–8
Purple loosestrife, or willow-herb	*Lythrum Salicaria*	p, 7
Purple magnolia	*Magnolia liliflora*	s, 5
Purple ragwort	*Senecio elegans*	a, 6–7
Ragged robin	*Lychnis Flos-cuculi*	b, 5–10
Rasp-leav'd geranium	*Pelargonium Radula*	g.
Rose cockle, or campion	*Lychnis Coronaria*	a, 5–7
Rose geranium	*Pelargonium graveolens*	g.
Rose vervain	*Verbena canadensis*	p, 6
*Sago palm	*Cycas revoluta*	g.
Scarlet fuchsia	*Fuchsia magellanica*	g, 2–10
Scarlet lychnis, or Maltese cross	*Lychnis chalcedonica*	p, 5–8
Scarlet monarda, or Oswego tea	*Monarda didyma*	p, 6–7
*Scotch broom	*Cytisus scoparius*	s, 5
Scots, or pheasant's-eye pink	*Dianthus plumarius*	p, 5–9
Scots rose, or burnet	*Rosa spinosissima*	s, 5
Sea holly	*Eryngium amethystinum*	p, 6–8
Sessile trillium, or wakerobin	*Trillium sessile*	p, 5
*Shaddock	*Citrus maxima*	g, 3, 6
Siberian iris	*Iris sibirica*	p, 6
Siberian squill	*Scilla sibirica*	p, 4
Single catchfly	*Viscaria viscosa*	b, 5
Sneezewort	*Achillea Ptarmica*	p, 5–6
Snow-drop	*Galanthus nivalis*	p, 3–4
Snow-in-summer	*Cerastium tomentosum*	p, 5
*Sour, or Seville orange	*Citrus Aurantium*	g, 3, 6
Spanish blush mallow	*Lavatera trimestris*	a, 5–7
Spanish squill	*Scilla hispanicus*	p, 5
Spiked cockscomb	*Celosia spicata*	a, 8–10
Spring crocus	*Crocus vernus*	p, 3–4
Spring snow-flake	*Leucojum vernum*	p, 3–4

Square-leaved corn-flag	*Gladiolus tristis*	a, 6
Stokes' aster	*Stokesia laevis*	p, 6–8
Stonecrop, or wallpepper	*Sedum acre*	p, 4
Strawflower	*Helichrysum bracteatum*	a, 7–9
Summer adonis, or pheasant's-eye	*Adonis aestivalis*	a, 6
*Summer perennial phlox	*Phlox paniculata*	p, 6
Sundrops, or evening primrose	*Œnothera fruticosa*	p, 6–7
Superb hibiscus	*Hibiscus coccineus*	p, 7–9
Sweet alyssum, or madwort	*Lobularia maritima*	a, 5–9
*Sweet bay	*Laurus nobilis*	g.
Sweet orange	*Citrus sinensis*	g, 3, 6
Sweet scabious, or mourning bride	*Scabiosa atropurpurea*	a, 5–8
Sweet sultan	*Centaurea moschata*	a, 5–7
Sweet william	*Dianthus barbatus*	b, 5–6
Sweet william catchfly	*Silene Armeria*	a, 5
Sweet wivelsfield	*Dianthus carthusianorum*	b, 5–6
Sweet violet	*Viola odorata*	p, 4–5
Tall browallia	*Browallia demissa*	a, 6
Tansy	*Tanacetum vulgare*	p, 6–7
Tawny day-lily	*Hemerocallis fulva*	p, 5–6
*Thready Adam's needle	*Yucca filamentosa*	p, 6–7
Three-coloured chrysanthemum	*Chrysanthemum tricolor*	a, 6–9
Three-leaved vervain, or lemon verbena	*Aloysia triphylla*	g, 7–10
Tickseed, annual	*Coreopsis tinctoria*	a, 6–9
Tickseed, perennial	*Coreopsis grandiflora*	p, 6–7
Tree crassula, or jade plant	*Crassula arborescens*	g, 2
Tuberose	*Polianthes tuberosa*	a, 7–9
Tulips, Garden	*Tulipa Gesneriana*	b,
Bybloem Varieties:		
Gala Beauty, or Columbus (1620)		4–5
Hautesse (1750)		5
La Mere Brune (1750)		5
Reine de Bresil (1780)		5
Reine des Fleurs (1780)		5
Cottage Variety:		
Zomerschoen (1620)		5

Double Early-Flowering Varieties:

    Couronne D'Or (1770)   4

    Tournesol Red and Yellow (1769)   4

Double Late-Flowering Varieties:

    Mariage de ma Fille (1750)   5

    Yellow Rose (1700)   5

Parrot Variety:

    Lutea major (1680)   5

Single Early-Flowering Varieties:

    Cramoisi Brilliant (1785)   4–5

    Keizerkroon, or Grand Duc (1750)   5

    Pottebaker Yellow (1760)   4–5

    Royal Standard (1760)   4–5

    Silver Standard (1760)   4–5

    Yellow Prince (1750)   4–5

Common name	Botanical name	Type, month
Turkish corn-flag	Gladiolus byzantinus	p, 5–6
Turk's-cap lily	Lilium Martagon	p, 6
Variegated iris	Iris variegata	p, 5
Violet-coloured zinnia	Zinnia elegans	a, 8–10
Virginia lungwort, cowslip or bluebells	Mertensia virginica	p, 4
Virginian flag	Iris versicolor	p, 6
Wallflower	Cheiranthus Cheiri	b, 4–7
White, or madonna lily	Lilium candidum	p, 6
White rose	Rosa alba	s, 5
*Wild sweet william, or early-flowering lychnidea	Phlox divaricata	p, 5
Winter aconite	Eranthis hyemalis	p, 2–4
Woolly milfoil	Achillea tomentosa	p, 6–7
Woolly woundwort, or lambs-ears	Stachys lanata	p, 5
Yarrow, or milfoil	Achillea Millefolium	p, 6–7
Yellow alyssum, or basket-of-gold	Alyssum saxatile	b, 4–5
Yellow and green tulip	Tulipa viridiflora	b, 5
Yellow day-lily	Hemerocallis lilio-asphodelus	p, 5–6
Yellow marsh flower-de-luce	Iris Pseudacorus	p, 5–6
Yellow meadowrue	Thalictrum flavum	p, 6–7

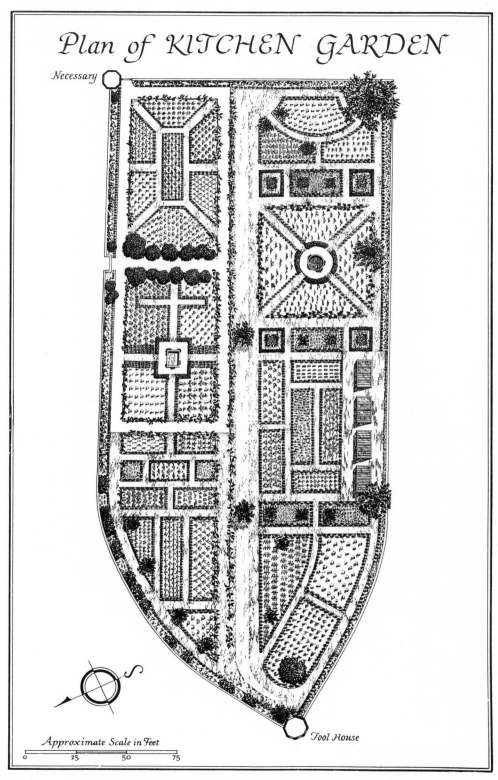

Plan of KITCHEN GARDEN

Necessary

Tool House

Approximate Scale in Feet

0   25   50   75

Figure 10. George Washington's original plan for the kitchen garden at Mount Vernon.

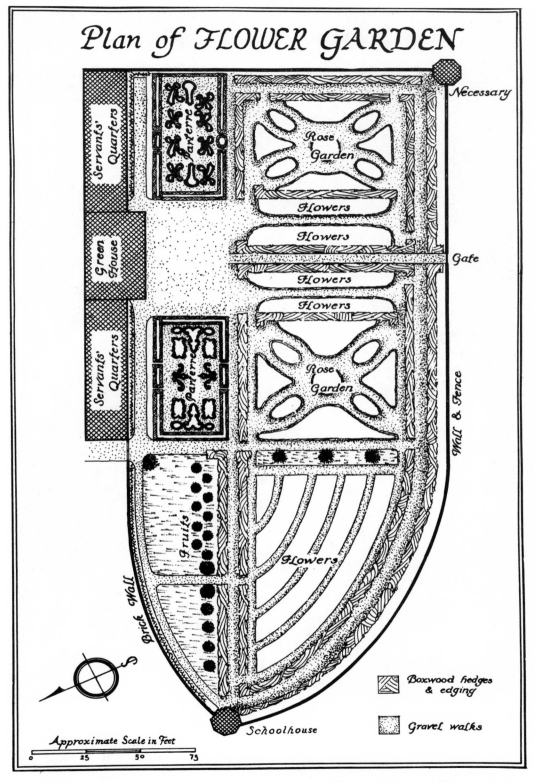

Figure 11. Plan of Flower Garden.

Figure 12. François Boucher's painting presents Madame Bergeret in the fashionable mode of the day with crisp silk, bows, frills, jewels and the beloved roses, still "chic," fragile and charming in the typical idyllic rococo setting. Reproduced through the courtesy of the National Gallery of Art, Washington, D.C., Samuel H. Kress Collection.

LOUIS XV PERIOD (1715–74) *Rococo*

Although historically this style was the extreme development of the ideas, individuality, imagination and love of broken curves that characterized baroque art, it was nevertheless a French original.

During the Regency and in the reign of Louis XV, court life was no longer regimented by strict rules of etiquette and the sharp eye of the old king. Paris, as well as Versailles, was the scene of cultural and social life in which women played an important role.

This was a period of great cultural and artistic attainment. It has been called the "age of reason," with the artistic expression one of cultivated and refined taste, playful charm, gaiety, brilliance and wit.

The rococo style in the decorative arts, as in all art, reflected the mood of the times. The finest talents were employed to produce a novel form of decoration of such perfection that French design was copied in the courts of all Europe—and has had a number of revivals.

This style was marked by a light, playful C-curve, ending in a delicate turned back scroll, a shortened double curve, rather than the heavier, bold S-curve of the baroque. The style *rocaille* comes from the sea, having a wavelike motion. Colors were the deep, cool blue of the sea and the whiteness of foam, combined with the rosy tint inside the mussel shell and the gleam of mother-of-pearl. These harmonies can be seen in the paintings of Boucher. Other color harmonies included light blue, deep blue, rose, pale and golden yellow, violet, white, soft greens, and blue-greens; and accents of Chinese red, as seen in the paintings of Fragonard, Nattier, Watteau, Lemoyne, and in the Beauvais tapestries.

The apartments consisted of smaller, more intimate rooms elaborately decorated and comfortably furnished. The panel mountings were delicately modeled ornaments with the backgrounds painted in soft colors, the detail gilded or silvered. Frequently, the panels were painted by the best artists of the day—N. Lancret, C. Huet, F. Boucher—with scenes of idealized peasant life, groups and landscapes in the Chinese taste, or birds and flowers. Ceilings were similarly painted and crystal chandeliers were hung. Furniture was lighter in weight than the massive pieces of the Louis XIV period and made in ensembles. The fantastic skill of the craftsmen was apparent in the floral marquetry, patterned veneer and ormolu mounts. Sofas and chairs were covered with tapestry of beautiful design.

It was the perfect taste and influence of Madame de Pompadour that contributed much to the excellence of this style. Under the patronage of this remarkable woman, the mistress of Louis XV, who exemplified the spirit of the time, many of the arts flourished. The silk mills at Lyons and the factories at Sèvres prospered through her efforts, and French

Figure 13. A lovely, definitely French bouquet from a wall panel by the Fragonard school. The delicacy and sprightliness of the design of favorite roses is typically rococo in feeling. Reproduced through the courtesy of the Corcoran Gallery of Art, Washington, D.C.

excavations at Herculaneum and Pompeii were encouraged through funds she secured.

Most beautiful, artistic vases of soft-paste porcelain were made at Vincennes and later at Sèvres gilded and painted with the motifs in vogue. The ground colors were rich—apple-green, turquoise-blue, rose-Pompadour and later dark blue. White porcelain with garlands of appliqué flowers were also popular, as were Chinese celadon vases with ormolu mountings. Round bowls, jardinieres and urns of metal and marble, gold mounted crystal vases, tazza with stems of dolphin or figures, and elaborate epergnes were the fashion.

Flower arrangements were smaller in scale in the more intimate salons and boudoirs where they were placed on mantels and small tables and pedestals. The designs in tall containers were sometimes the height of the container and sometimes twice the height. Fewer large flowers were used and these were grouped gracefully without crowding, but light and airy in feeling. Many smaller flowers, buds, graceful sprays, slender, swirling foliage and tendrils added to the charm and provided the delicate, turned-back scroll. Arrangements for gala fetes were more elaborate. Flowers were often combined with fruits in fantastic epergnes.

Flowers chosen for the arrangement in *Plate* 8 were of the colors and some of the kinds found in the design on the vase. Roses approximate in form the lovely cabbage rose so popular in France, and lilac, deutzia, delphinium, daffodils, windflower, pansies, roses, Christmas rose, daisies, strawflowers, love-in-a-mist, single hyacinth and hydrangea were used. Delicate foliage of trumpet vine and grape tendrils have the reverse C-curve form which was characteristic of the rococo style. The container is a Sèvres vase of somewhat later period with a ground color of Pompadour pink.

Figure 14. The Creil reproduction container with the idealized peasant scene motif sets the period as Louis XV. A small bouquet of almost Pompadour-pink roses and pastel blues and white, and the sprightly outline add to the rococo spirit.

Classic Revival   LATE GEORGIAN PERIOD (1762–1830)
Style

This new style, a product of the genius of Robert Adam, was quickly and enthusiastically accepted. Studies of the ruins of Diocletian's great palace in Dalmatia, and buildings in Rome inspired the creation of this classical style of the highest charm and distinction adapted from classical models.

Not only did he build houses but decorated and furnished them as well, making the Adam drawing room a unique product of English art.

Adam designed furniture, but it was Hepplewhite and Sheraton who produced it for these rooms. The most obvious features of the style were the formal symmetry, the slender proportions and the delicate scale of molding. Garlands, fan patterns, urns, wreaths, paterae and honeysuckle were the favorite motifs. Elaborately molded stucco decorations of the ceilings, employing circles or ovals and half circles, and classical figures, contributed to the effect of genteel elegance.

Decorative panels were painted by the German artist Angelica Kauffmann and included garlands and baskets of small blossoms. In Gobelin tapestries, designed for Adam rooms, can be seen classic urns filled with large bouquets of roses, peonies, poppies and sprays of foliage amid garlands and swags.

Colors were pale and cool and used in restricted color schemes—white and gold, ivory and dead-white, misty-blue with silver or cream, steel-gray with white, moss-green and ivory. Strong notes of color were introduced for mantelpieces, sculpture and decorative urns.

Wedgwood containers imitating the shapes of the Greek pieces were perfect creations for the Adam rooms, as were jasperware vases with classic figures and leaves of fine relief designs. Classic urns of marble and alabaster, as well as oval, elliptical or boat-shaped footed silver containers and low baskets were favored.

A late Georgian flower arrangement to grace an Adam drawing room would be elegantly formal and symmetrically balanced, possessing a delicate lightness.

The green-and-white arrangement in *Plate* 9 exhibits the stateliness, symmetry, formality and grace of the Adam style. Roses, peonies and tulips make up the design within the triangular form. Double larkspur and deutzia radiate to form a precise yet interesting and delicate outline. Lilac and hydrangea are transitional material. Love-in-a-mist, achillea (the Pearl), daffodils and rosebuds add variety. The white effect of flowers and vase is set off by the striking green peony foliage.

PLATE 1. The classic wreath and the Italian baroque bouquet styles are combined in a two-tiered wicker basket. The arrangement was created as Ferrari suggested, according to "one's preference, taste and imagination."

PLATE 2. An interpretation of Dutch-Flemish flower paintings. This arrangement appeared as part of an educational exhibit, "The History of Flower Arrangement," in the Garden Club Section of the National Capital Flower Show, in Washington, D. C., in 1969.

PLATE 3. Grandiose baroque elegance was the intent in the composition of this arrangement "in the manner of" the Louis XIV period.

PLATE 4. A restrained use of the baroque style, inspired by Jacob van Huysum's flower paintings, for the English taste of the Early Georgian period.

PLATE 5. An Early Colonial bouquet of mixed field flowers.

PLATE 6. A colorful style reflects the beauty of the Palladian drawing room of Gunston Hall, an historic house of the Colonial Georgian period in Virginia. Arranged by Mrs. Jack C. Fuson.

PLATE 7. This arrangement in the baroque style stands on the "hunt board" in the wide hall at Gunston Hall, the Colonial Georgian plantation home of George Mason.

PLATE 8. Rococo delicacy and sprightliness "in the French manner of the Louis XV period."

PLATE 9. This elegantly formal arrangement would aptly grace an Adam drawing room of the Late-Georgian period. Arranged by Mrs. Robert W. Wheat.

PLATE 10. An arrangement reminiscent of Prévost's flower paintings of the Louis XVI period. The blue-black glass vase of classic shape holds flowers in a flame-like form.

PLATE 11. An imposing classic revival urn sets the style of the Directoire period and holds an arrangement so French in feeling.

PLATE 12. An arrangement after the flower paintings of Anne Vallayer-Coster, Empire period, France.

LOUIS XVI PERIOD (1774–92)

The classic revival in France was inspired by the discovery of Pompeii and Herculaneum.

A more restrained decoration, based on straight lines, right angles, ovals and circles arranged in symmetrical design replaced the sinuous baroque and rococo forms.

Figure 15. The tall basket, or Greek calathos, filled with flowers was a favorite motif of the classic revival style appearing in tapestries and wall panels. It was, however, an early favorite for this detail from the Gobelin tapestry, "Diana," is after a design by Claude Audran (c. 1700). Reproduced through the courtesy of the Corcoran Gallery of Art, Washington, D.C.

Though the same decorating technique was used, new motifs from classical sources appeared: palmettes, tripod stands, classical figures, thyrsi, trophies of arms, lyres, arabesques and vases—amphora, cornucopia and baskets—filled with flowers.

Furniture was made with straight lines in rectangular proportions. The cabriole leg disappeared, and straight, slender tapered legs took their place, and the gilded decoration was of classical design.

Artists and craftsmen took great pleasure in the use of the new form. Exquisite work was produced in all the arts and copied in every corner of Europe.

Hard-paste porcelain vases were produced at Vincennes, Limoges, Orléans and Paris, along with the continued production of soft-paste at Sèvres. Style of vases changed from rococo to more classical forms and decorations.

Figure 16. A pair of little bouquets only seven inches high in classic two-handled urns of moss-green marked with gold. Pink roses, yellow goldenrod and strawflowers with delicate maidenhair fern make a lovely pastel color harmony. Arranged by Lurena Mae Shank.

Flower arrangements themselves were little changed; flowers do not lend themselves to rigid classical lines. They were, however, arranged in vases of classical form and decoration. A flower painting by Gerard van Spaëndonck, a Dutch painter at the Court of Louis XVI, is very much like those seen in the baroque style, but it stands on a pedestal of classical style. In a portrait of Marie Antoinette by Mme. Vigée-Lebrun, there appears a lovely arrangement in a tall crystal vase with gold mountings in which spike flowers have more prominence than seen in flower compositions of earlier periods. Colors were similar to those of the rococo period. Turquoise blue was a favorite color of Marie Antoinette.

Lilac gained popularity and was used along with roses, delphinium and flowers of the former period.

Anne Vallayer-Coster and Jean-Louis Prévost were both noted for their flower paintings during this period as well as in the Directoire and Empire periods.

The arrangement in *Plate 10* was composed "in the manner of" the flower paintings of Jean-Louis Prévost (1760–1810) who became a member of the Académie Saint Luc in 1791. His mixed bouquets of restrained triangular form were painted with a French feeling for the lightness and fragility of flowers, but did not appear in vases. The handsome container chosen for this style has the slender classic proportions characteristic of the furniture of this period. Flowers are those favored by the artist: roses, lilac and anemone. Verbena was included as a substitute for the auricula, and sprays of young rose foliage are lovely.

DIRECTOIRE PERIOD (1795–99)

Much of the elegance of the Louis XVI style survived the revolution. Flower arrangements were little changed in this period but certain types of vases were characteristic. In Figure 14, the Creil container bears a classic motif often referred to as "directoire ladies." The tall imposing black marble urn in *Plate 11* was a very fashionable type often used in pairs for purely ornamental purposes.

The handsome classic urn in *Plate 11* holds flowers of the more fashionable colors of the Directoire Period: powder-blue delphinium, dusty-pink tulips and roses, lime-green helleborus, rose carnations, lilac, pale blue Dutch iris, lavender stokesia, white loosestrife, dull red anemone, blue columbine and sage-green Baker's fern.

Figure 17. A lovely small decorative piece of delicate color harmony. Some of the most charming dried flowers were used: roses in various shades of pink, white lilac, pale blue and deeper blue delphinium, the white achillea—the pearl—dainty white sprays of deutzia, blue cornflower, pink and ivory strawflowers, blue and white love-in-a-mist, and soft green trumpet vine and rose foliage. Arranged by Mrs. Robert W. Wheat.

EMPIRE PERIOD (1804–14)

The decorating style of this period was greatly influenced by Napoleon's dreams of rivaling Caesar and the antiquities of Rome, Greece and Egypt. Styles in interior decoration and furnishings became heavy and pompous.

The Empress Josephine, in her garden at Malmaison, grew all the known roses. Pierre-Joseph Redouté, the court artist, has more than a thousand rose and lily paintings to his credit, all beautifully painted in compact bouquets but not placed in vases.

Vases were patterned after severely classic urns. The Sèvres factory produced many pairs of emerald-green, royal-blue and turquoise ground colors, hand-painted with flowers and scenes and decorated with gold. Vases of classic form with Empire motifs were made at other factories as well. Marble and alabaster urns were also in vogue.

Although heavy compact arrangements in classic urns of rich colors would be appropriate for this period, an arrangement "in the manner of" the flower paintings of Anne Vallayer-Coster (1744–1818) was chosen. She was noted for her flower paintings, which were informal, compact, substantial bouquets of beautifully painted flowers. Blues, whites, soft pinks, orange-reds, deep reds and dark purples were composed with colors spotted rather than with easy transition. Her containers were sturdy vase shapes, sometimes footed.

The container in *Plate 12* was of a type used not only by Anne Vallayer-Coster but also in the Dutch-Flemish period and in the earlier French periods. Flowers used are roses, lilac, delphinium, larkspur, daffodils, pansies, marigolds, love-in-a-mist, poppy foliage and seed pods, hyacinth, celosia and dahlias (not a flower of the period but right in color and form).

FEDERAL PERIOD (1789–1820)   *Classic Revival Style, America (1785–1865)*

The baroque style of the Colonial Georgian period was replaced by the classic revival during the years in which the Federal government and its institutions were established.

Thomas Jefferson was the first and chief exponent of the new classicism, exerting his influence in the selection of architects, and was largely responsible for commissioning the French officer-engineer, Pierre Charles L'Enfant, to create the master plan for the new Federal city, a plan of classic flavor with a definite French accent. The foremost Federal-style mansion in the Washington-Philadelphia area was, appropriately enough, the White House, designed by James Hoban.

Although interiors of houses of this style were similar, regional differences were evident. The most subtle and refined interpretation of the Adam style appeared in New England in the work of Samuel McIntire. A continental splendor predominated in New York and the central states with aspects of the oncoming Empire style newly arrived from France. An air of aristocratic elegance distinguished the beautiful mansions of the South.

The qualities that characterized the Federal style are striking in their differences when compared to the baroque. There was greater formality and the scale of the interior decoration was more delicate, possessing a simplified elegance. In the adaptation of the Adam style, walls were unadorned and painted in light tones, grayed tints or white, with pure white woodwork setting off the rich colored draperies and upholstery. High ceilings were decorated with molded stucco patterns that tended to be centered designs. Decorative emphasis was concentrated on the mantel and overmantel, cornices, doors and window frames, enriched by

Adam-inspired delicate repeat ornament. In general, geometric forms had their embodiment in the urn, swag, paterae and wreath in fine scale and delicate precision.

The taste for lightness was reflected in the furniture. The designs of George Hepplewhite and Thomas Sheraton, and the Louis XVI and Directoire forms, influenced American cabinetmakers. American versions were produced by Samuel McIntire of Salem, John Seymour of Boston, Duncan Phyfe of New York, Henry Connelly of Philadelphia, and the excellent cabinet shops of Baltimore and Charleston. Light woods and finishes and decorative inlays were characteristic.

Information on flower arrangement in this period is so meager that the style must be interpreted from precedents and also settings—in this case, the Diplomatic Reception Rooms of the Department of State in Washington, D.C. These rooms are in frequent use for official functions where foreign diplomats and American guests are entertained by the Secretary of State. Americans can be proud of these rooms for in them are displayed and used noteworthy examples of American eighteenth-century and early nineteenth-century decorative arts and furnishings, many of historical significance. It is through the efforts of the Special Fine Arts Committee's "Project Americana" that the rooms are being furnished by gifts and loans from public-spirited citizens.

The John Quincy Adams State Drawing Room is furnished in Colonial Georgian style, in the manner of an elegant American drawing room of the late eighteenth century. The room might well be called the "American Chippendale" room as that style predominates. Foreign visitors are often amazed that works of art of such perfection and sophistication were produced by American artist-craftsmen during that period of our history.

The flower arrangement in this room, seen in *Plate 13*, stands beneath the portrait of Martha Washington, by Rembrandt Peale, on a unique Philadelphia Chippendale fret-carved side table by Thomas Afflect (c. 1760). It was created with sensitivity to the magnificence of the decor and also as a transitional piece. The white porcelain classic urn is decorated with the American eagle motif so proudly used during the early period of the new republic. The flowers are composed with restraint to give the large pyramidal mass a feeling of formality, elegance and lightness. The reds of the roses and celosia were selected to echo the beautiful shade of the scarlet silk brocade on the Chippendale settees across the room. The large single pink peonies contribute to the distinction of the arrangement, while the daintier flowers add to its charm.

The James Monroe Reception Room and the James Madison Dining Room comprise a private suite for use by the Secretary of State for official functions attended by a small number of guests. They are being furnished in the Federal style with rare pieces by noted American cabinet-makers in the Hepplewhite, Sheraton and Duncan Phyfe styles. Since the classic revival style rarely appeared in America until after the Revolution, the wave of patriotism that swept the country at that time motivated the use of inlay motifs of the eagle and the Great Seal of the United States as decorative devices on chairs, cupboards, tables and sideboards.

The arrangement in the James Monroe Reception Room in *Plate 14* was made to pick up the colors of the fabrics on the Duncan Phyfe settees, of rust-red, gold and beige. The container is a Chinese export bowl decorated with the favorite American eagle motif.

GREEK REVIVAL PERIOD (1820–50)

Just as at the turn of the century Rome had provided the symbol for republican enthusiasm, now ancient Greece seemed synonymous with democratic ideals. The Greek temple facades with colonnaded porticos became the favored style. Banks, churches, city halls, schools and mansions stood in city after city with Greek names: Athens, Sparta, Troy.

Benjamin Latrobe, a friend of Thomas Jefferson, helped to launch the Greek revival, and his student Robert Mills, who designed the Washington Monument, also designed a number of homes in his native city of Charleston, South Carolina, and in Baltimore and Savannah. The vast plantation mansions of the South with their colonnaded porticos varied tremendously but remained the dominant style until the Civil War.

Furnishings and draperies were in the heavier Sheraton-Empire taste.

The arrangement in *Plate 15* is a yellow-and-white compact mound of Shasta daisies, goldenrod and ferns.

EMPIRE PERIOD (1830–50)

Stimulated by the Empire style of France and by the emerging Caesars of industry and commerce and by archeological exploration, the designers combined Pompeiian, Greek, Roman and Egyptian elements to create imposing and grand interiors. There was increased weight, and the delicacy of proportion that distinguished the turn-of-the-century decor was gone, replaced by heavier, massive and monumental furniture. Classical columns were incorporated into the pier table, marble and brass or ormolu were combined with gleaming varnished mahogany wood, the use of animal and human forms—sphinxes, phoenixes, claw feet and eagle heads—all contributed to an imposing imperial effect. An amazing number of small objects were introduced—mirrors, wall sconces, candelabra, urns, pitchers, vases, elaborate clocks. Heavy colors replaced the pale or bright sharp colors of the previous years. Duncan Phyfe used remarkable taste in using elements of the Empire style; in the hands of lesser men a decline in taste was evident.

Containers would have shown these same tendencies.

In *Plate 16* the dark red of the roses and prince's feather celosia, and the brown glycerine-treated laurel foliage carry the colors of the Empire-style urn through the arrangement. Queen Elizabeth and tropicana roses are contrasting colors in the polychromatic scheme. Dahlias provide new areas of interest. Goldenrod, lilac and larkspur are transitional material giving grace to the silhouette, while Persian jewel zinnias and acroclinium are contrasting forms. The Queen Anne's lace relieves the weight of the heavy mass.

The Romantic Period (1830–90)

In this era of progress, success, money and expansion there still existed romantic sentiments, and great enthusiasm for nature, science, education, new machines, social reform and cultural development. This period can be viewed from sufficient distance today to make it possible to appreciate a certain charm in many of the fashions and a feeling of sympathetic amusement for some of the fads.

By 1835 the restraints of classicism had grown tedious, and social and economic changes, already initiated by the Industrial Revolution, encouraged reaction. Emotional and romantic aspirations were expressed in a series of styles ill-adapted to actual conditions. The Greek revival was diluted almost immediately by the Gothic, setting the stage for the novel and exotic in decorative taste created by a wealth-induced appetite for comfort and display. A heavy, ornate, crowded confusion resulted when decorative motifs and objects were easily and cheaply produced by machine. At mid-century a coarsened "second rococo" triumphed, succeeded by the heavier baroque and Renaissance.

This was not only the American taste, but the European as well; indeed, it was Queen Victoria after whom the period style is often called.

Rooms became crowded with furniture often upholstered with patterned fabrics, and toward the end of the century, in the French taste, with plush and fringe. Brightly colored wallpapers in bold patterns covered the walls, and patterned carpets on the floors vied for attention. Fireplaces were often mounted with elaborate overmantels fitted with mirror panels and a multitude of shelves and brackets for the display of Victorian knickknacks. White plaster ceilings with modeled cornices had some central feature, usually a lighting fixture of gaudy rococo design.

Charles Eastlake wrote a book in vigorous protest against the Victorian taste, which was published in England in 1866 and in America in 1872. He made an appeal to have materials treated in such a way as to reveal their essential character, and to have design grow from the function that heralds the coming style. William Morris (1834–96) formed a school dominated by his protest against machine production, while

Figure 18. The Blue Room at the White House is barely recognizable under the plethora of ornament and decoration in fashion at the turn of the century. Reproduced from the Frances Benjamin Johnston Collection, by courtesy of the Prints and Photographs Division of the Library of Congress (LC-J698, 81303 and 81311).

Figure 19. A lithograph by N. Currier, belonging to the author, exemplifies one type of Victorian bouquet: a fanciful container in blue and gold, a compact mass with a lightened silhouette, flowers with patterned form, and a color combination of ashes-of-roses, mauve, dull red, green and white.

seeking to turn back to natural forms, pure color and good hand crafts-manship. Neither of these movements had widespread influence.

The amount of information on flower arrangement styles in this period, unlike, some others, is almost overwhelming. Paintings, flower paintings, lithographs, photographs and "fancywork" designs show innumerable com-positions. Magazines of the day, such as *Godey's Lady's Book* and *St. Nicholas*, were filled with advice and suggestions on growing and ar-ranging flowers. Julia S. Berrall, in her book, *A History of Flower Ar-rangement*, gives interesting and detailed accounts from these sources. Young ladies were encouraged to paint flowers, embroider them, model them in wax, or to create fanciful forms from wool or shells to be proudly displayed under glass domes. A romantic symbolism was attached to flowers. Tussie-mussies or nosegays were made to speak the "language of flowers," and little books were published to make this new language intelligible.

Most of the kinds of flowers known today were in cultivation at the beginning of the period, but great work in hybridization produced many new varieties. Much was accomplished to improve the size, form and color of flowers that Ferrari dreamed of in seventeenth-century Italy. Some new introductions were azaleas, camellias, new varieties of chrys-anthemums, nandina, forsythia, petunias, verbena, deutzia and dahlias. The Victorian taste was for variegated and streaked flowers, patterned and unique and drooping forms, such as honeycombed dahlias with streaked or tipped markings, spotted calceolaria, speckled lilies, striped salpiglossis, pansies with cunning faces, fuchsias (called lady's eardrops), bleeding-hearts, variegated carnations, stephanotis, geraniums—especially the *Pelargonium*—striped and feathery grasses, and ferns, such as aspara-gus, *Adiantum* and Boston.

Favorite colors were magenta, purple, mauve, mustard-yellow, ashes-of-roses and red.

Containers of every imaginable kind were turned out by the hundreds in Europe and America. Fine porcelains in rococo, baroque, Chinese and classic shapes, exquisitely hand-painted, were produced by the better fac-tories in England, France and Germany. Ambitious specimens were ex-hibited at "The Great Exhibition of the Works of Industry of all Nations," held in the Crystal Palace in London in 1851, and at smaller exhibitions throughout the nineteenth century. Many of these pieces can be seen in museum galleries. Fantastic shapes grossly ornamented with painted and applied designs were also produced all over Europe and in America. White Parian ware, the new ceramic and a great favorite, was made in America at the Bennington factory in Vermont. After 1880 Rookwood

Figure 20. The flower design on the vase was carried into the arrangement with pink roses, mauve dahlias, bronze strawflowers, yellow snapdragon, purple-blue delphinium, button zinnias, and blue globe thistle. Larkspur tips and maidenhair fern give airiness to the outline.

Figure 21. A small mound of pastel colors in a hobnail glass pitcher is a lovely decorative piece for a small table. Dainty flowers are roses, statice, larkspur, hydrangea, globe amaranth, strawflowers, pompon dahlias and maidenhair fern. Arranged by Lurena Mae Shank.

and Weller factories in Zanesville, Ohio, turned out most artistic pottery vases.

Glass vases, whether pressed, cut or engraved, were widely manufactured in America and Europe. They were often wonderfully colorful in opaline, satin glass, ruby, violet, bottle-green, pink luster and milk glass. Epergnes were terribly fashionable with the spout type leading the list. Perhaps this was the best way to make a bouquet conspicuous in the crowded rooms.

The composition of Victorian arrangements was prim and contrived, often an almost round compact mass, the outline relieved with rococo sprightliness through the use of delicate sprays and buds, slender leaves and often drooping and trailing flowers and foliage.

The design on the Limoges-type vase in *Plate* 17 was repeated as to flowers and colors in the arrangement. Favorites of the period were used: roses, dahlias, carnations, striped tulips, strawflowers, everlasting pea, larkspur, pansies and maidenhair fern.

Sentiments and "busy" work made "ghost" bouquets of skeletonized leaves popular. Dried arrangements were also in vogue. Bunches of pampas grass and honesty were as popular as peacock feathers; and everlastings, such as strawflowers, globe amaranth and statice, were combined with dainty grasses and seed pods.

It was in this period that the use of borax became popular as the exciting new method for preserving flowers. (Today borax has been generally replaced by the new desiccant silica gel and the incomparable sand-drying method first described by Ferrari in seventeenth-century Italy.)

House plants of many varieties—palms, dracaena, rubber plants, and especially ferns of all kinds—were used to decorate the already crowded room. Large estates had extensive conservatories where beautiful horticultural specimens were carefully grown. On special occasions entire walls were banked with plants. In appraising these fashions, one must surmise that the Victorians would have disdained the plastic substitutes of today.

The French flower painters of the nineteenth century reveal a new and glowing character. Gustave Courbet's flowers were naturalistic and casual. Édouard Manet's were of aesthetic importance, rich, vivid masses of color in designs both conservative and revolutionary. Colors in Claude Monet's paintings were pure colors vibrating in light. Henri Fantin-Latour understood flowers, their growth and delicacy of form, and painted them for their own beauty and also with vibrant color in surrounding light. The arrangements of Paul Cézanne and Vincent van Gogh, as well as Manet and Fantin-Latour, are considered to belong more to the twentieth

Figure 22. "Zinnias in a Blue Vase." Inspired by French impressionistic flower paintings.

century than the nineteenth. Renoir, on the other hand, painted some bouquets reminiscent of the rococo style. Odilon Redon's flowers were mysterious, and he also painted in the Art Nouveau style.

Art Nouveau *(1890–1910)*   Artists, especially in France, turned back to nature for the essence of form and, influenced by Japanese art, created an original style. Their art was based on fluid forms and twisting, interlacing lines that were the quintessence of fire, wind and water. These motifs appeared in a "whip-lash" linearism or chessboard or lozenge form. All art forms from furniture, architecture, jewelry, textiles, to sculpture and painting were so influenced.

Arts and crafts shops under a number of artists sprang up all over Europe, with a passion for good craftsmanship and a tendency for artists to express their talents in interior decorations in their own homes in a unified concept.

Many vases were made in bold, unusual shapes. Polychrome glass was a favorite medium. Emile Gallé, who formed a school at Nancy, France, manufactured tall vases with striking flower or insect surface decorations. René Lalique created heavy, low, wide bowls with intricate surface designs. Louis Tiffany in New York designed some of his vases after a flower—the bulb, the stem and the unfolding corolla. Work was in harmony with the plant-obsessed spirit of the style. Porcelain and pottery vases were also made with new shapes and decorations, and the compound trumpet epergne was used for table arrangements.

In one of his flower paintings, Odilon Redon (1840–1916) used a tall, tubular vase with undulating lines as a decorative pattern in which black-centered anemone appeared in a low mound as concentric circles. This mass was lightened by short sprays of baby's breath. The whole effect was new and revolutionary.

The colors for this style were cool or warm, not vivid or intense, but dull, grayed and muted. Iridescent peacock-feather colors, dull silver and opalescent gold colors were widely used.

In *Plate* 18, the slender opalescent container (carnival glass) holds a misty spray of flax seed pods with Mexicana zinnias, tulips, dahlias, and glycerine-treated crabapple foliage "in the manner of" a flower painting by Redon.

Artistic changes were in evidence before the turn of the century, but no new style was developed. Sophistication rather than sentimentality was the tone of the period for Edward VII was a genial man with world-wide interests and a zest for life.

The arrangement in *Plate 19* is similar in its silhouette to a mass-arrangement style often seen in England today; however, this composition is more compact and the rhythmic lines are not as free-flowing.

Step-by-step construction of this arrangement is illustrated under "Creating the Styles with Dried Flowers."

The Edwardian Period (1901–10)

In Japan, flower arranging, rich in tradition and symbolism, has been a recognized art for centuries and developed in many schools, of which *Ikenobo* is the oldest.

Ikebana

Rikkwa or *Rikka* (the word means standing flowers), the earliest classic style, evolved as a formal temple art. The large complicated structure of pyramidal form was constructed to suggest a natural landscape in its entirety. Foliage and flowers were selected to suggest symbolically each part of the entire picture—hills, valleys and water, near, far, vast and minute.

In the fifteenth century the classic style of the *Ikenobo* school, *Shoka*, emerged and reached near perfection in the eighteenth century. This style suggests the spirit rather than the semblance of a thing—an arrested moment of growth, the inherent beauty of a season, or a mood of nature inspired by a poem, or a remembered landscape.

Mastering the technique of the *Shoka* style is the first step in flower training in many Japanese schools. Patience, skill and knowledge of first principles are learned.

These designs are formed with three main lines, "heaven," "earth" and "man," or *ten-chi-jin*. The tallest line, "heaven" (*Shin*), is at least one and one-half times the height of the container. A gentle curving is forced into it if it does not possess one, and in order to obtain perfect balance the tip of the branch must appear directly over the spot where the stem emerges from the container. The "man" line (*Soe*) should be two-thirds the length of the *Shin* line, while the "earth" line (*Tai*) is two-thirds the length of *Soe*.

Three aspects of expression appear in flower arrangement, as in other Japanese art—formal, semi-formal and informal. These aspects apply to the flowers and foliage, vases and bases, and to the materials from which they are made as well.

This classic style is of three main types. *Shin* is formal and upright, tall,

伊吹
ぎんか

Figure 23. Style of the *Ko-ryu* school of the nineteenth century, characterized by the use of two kinds of branches with exaggerated curving lines.

slender and of clear-cut lines and appears in upright vases of bronze or pottery. *Gyo* is semi-formal, made of gently curving, broader and more sweeping lines. Vases are upright of medium height, such as a usubata or a basket. *So* is informal with rather indeterminate contours with less stress on line or with sweeping lines of horizontal emphasis. Vases are varied and include low bronze and pottery, called *suibans*, bamboo cylinders (some double-tiered) and "boats" or "moons" of bamboo or pottery.

Figure 24. The *Nijyu-ike* bamboo container holds a traditional arrangement in the classic *Shoka* style. The *shin* line is winged euonymus, the *soe line is magnolia*, and celosia and fern form the *tai* line. Designer, Mrs. Paul E. Todd.

Many conventions regulate the selection of flowers and the techniques of arrangement. An illusion of growth (called *nemato*) is given by having all stems emerge from the container at the same point and extend together for four or five inches. Stems, foliage, buds and flowers are selected to spell out the entire character of a plant. The height relationship found in nature is observed and a tree branch is placed higher than a shrub or flower, and mountain plants are used above field flowers. Flowers are always used in season. Asymmetrical compositions are right- or left-handed according to their position at an altar on each side of an imaginary Buddha. The way in which flowers and foliage turn toward the sun is re-created with the viewer considered to be in the position of the sun.

Main characteristics are: A dynamic linear quality, asymmetrical balance, triangular form based on lines of related length, simplicity, clarity, restraint and subtle use of color.

By the early nineteenth century new schools employed exaggerated curving of lines and more than one kind of material. Two of these still in existence are the *Ko-ryu* and *Enshu-ryu*.

The *Nageire* style, naturalistic and informal, became popular in the sixteenth century. Zen Buddhism and the Tea Ceremony are largely responsible for its popularity and influenced the development of this style as it had that of the *Ikenobo* school.

For the Tea Ceremony a religious shrine, an alcove called *Tokonomo*, was built into one wall of a teahouse or special room. It held hanging scrolls, a flower arrangement and sometimes an art object or incense

Figure 25. *Nageire*, "throw-in" style, is pictured in this old print.

Figure 26. *Nageire,* "throw-in" style, (upper left) and *Moribana,* naturalistic style, (lower right).

burner. The *Tokonomo* was subsequently built into the Japanese home and held a place of high honor.

Nageire ("throw-in") is informal, of casual appearance, but sensitivity to plants and skill in design is needed to produce the artful effect of spontaneity.

Three main lines, "heaven," "man" and "earth," are used just as in the classical, but they may lean at an angle as in nature. The "heaven" and "man" lines may be foliage or fruit-tree branches, while the "earth" line may be made of flowers, or the whole arrangement may be made of flowers.

Three kinds of arrangements are standing, lateral or hanging.

Containers are tall or medium height, and may be of pottery, bamboo, baskets and wooden utensils.

Proportions vary—the "heaven" branch may be one and one-half times the height of the container and held by traditional stem holders.

The *Moribana* style, a twentieth-century development, is informal and

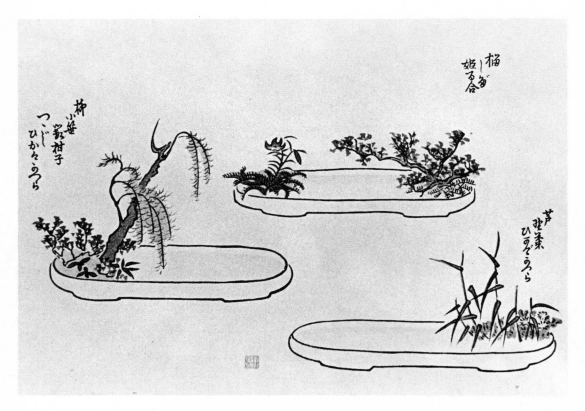

Figure 27. Prints showing the water-viewing style at center and lower left, and the naturalistic style at lower right.

naturalistic. Flat containers are always used and an expanse of water is always visible. Arrangements may suggest a natural scene with placement of flowers relevant to the seasonal mood. Western influence has brought about the use of cut flowers without branches and an emphasis on color.

Modern schools have broken with tradition, and dramatic, imaginative and ultra-modern arrangements are seen. Ikebana has become international. Some of the well-known schools are *Ohara, Sogetsu,* and *Ichyo.*

Long and devoted study is necessary for any real understanding of the art. Without training, arrangements are made only "in the manner of" Japanese styles.

Plate 20 shows an *Ichyo* line arrangement using *Corylus contorta* as the three main lines assisted by two red roses. Rocks of subtle colors cover the pin-point holder. The bronze usubata was designed by Meikoff Kasuya, the Headmaster of the Ichyo School.

A Japanese free-style design is shown in *Plate 21.* Scotch broom, deutzia and a single camellia blossom, of exotic color acquired in the

Figure 28. Lamb-ears and hydrangea in the unique water jug make a lovely color harmony of blue and gray in this Japanese free-style design. Designer, Mrs. Paul E. Todd

drying process, accentuate the color and shape of the handsome *Raku* container made by Jean Amos.

Some favorite material is:

Aspidistra	Cryptomeria	Peach
Aster	Grasses	Peony
Azalea	Hemlock	Pine
Bamboo	Hosta	Plum
Broom	Iris	Quince
Camellia	Juniper	Reeds
Cedar	Magnolia	Rose
Cherry	Maple	Willow
Chrysanthemum	Narcissus	Wisteria
	Orchid	

Contemporary American Style

In the changing world of today, new directions in intellectual concepts and social tendencies have led toward exploration and deeply felt expression in artistic life.

It was the famous Armory Show in New York in 1913 that made Americans generally aware of what was going on in the art world of Europe—a shocking and disturbing experience. To be so ushered into the twentieth century led to wide diversity in experimentation as an expression of those forces that make up the modern world.

There has been a growing trend to non-realistic styles in painting and sculpture; an alteration of natural shapes, proportions and colors in the interest of design or emotional expressiveness.

Modernism and functionalism in architecture had its beginnings with the Chicago architect, Louis Sullivan, and the Bauhaus movement which began in Germany in the 1920s. In interior decoration, the ornamental motifs of the past were disregarded and attention was directed to simplicity of form, texture and color. The rearrangement of interior space and bringing the outside in had a liberalizing effect. The "international style" of furniture and furnishings, an outcome of the functionalist movement in its direct approach to needs and material, is in complete opposition to the concepts of the Renaissance, which had completely dominated western design for the preceding four hundred years.

Changes in flower-arrangement styles to follow modern trends in art have been fostered by the national garden club organizations and Ikebana International. Schools, workshops and flower shows held under their tutelage have brought new concepts in flower arrangement as a visual art form. Exhibition work is imaginative, original and beautiful, or sometimes outlandish.

Garden clubs have placed emphasis not only on flower arrangement but also on horticultural practice, conservation and beautification. One wonders if the new attitudes required to solve the ecological problems of today may again emphasize the feeling of identity with nature begun in the Romantic movement by Rousseau. What will be the new direction in flower arrangement?

The modernistic style is ever new-fashioned for it is developed to break with tradition and the familiar. Interpretive styles express an idea, mood or theme. One type often referred to as Modern is an imaginative design with materials placed realistically. Free style is a personal expression partially freed from traditional patterns. Abstract is an expression in pure form, color, line and texture using plant material in unrealistic ways.

Traditional styles—line, mass and massed-line—are still in fashion. Their decorative value is especially important in homes with period furnishings and for those of mixed styles. Arrangements may be created to be reminiscent of the past but are more interesting with a fresh interpretation to please the modern eye.

There is a new approach to the selection of plant material for flower arrangement today. Not only is there an appreciation of the beauty of flowers, but arrangers are discovering marvelous unexpected materials everywhere in nature. Bare branches and vines appear as lively rhythms—sweeping, gently curving or twisting. Pieces of driftwood or weathered wood and stone appear as fantastic natural sculpture. Foliage is now emphasized for its shapes, patterns and textures. Seed vessels can be grotesque, unusual or sometimes elegant forms. Sensivity to color makes it the most exciting of all the elements of design, and the strong emotional appeal of color opens many avenues for artistic effects.

Dried and/or treated plant materials are amazingly modern and most effectively used in all types of designs. Naturally dried material can be collected in field and forest, on the seashore or desert, in the garden or the mountains. An awareness of beauty because of a sensitive way of seeing makes selection an exciting adventure. This material can be combined with preserved flowers and foliage. The value of distinctive dried material has been recognized by the garden clubs and Ikebana International and is welcomed for use in certain classes in flower shows. The National Council of State Garden Clubs offers the "Award of Distinction" in a Standard Flower Show for the blue-ribbon winner selected from a designated group of classes in which the exhibits must consist of dried and/or treated plant material.

Containers of every type and kind are available: fine antiques from around the world, good reproductions and modern styles of porcelain, metal, pottery, glass and stone. Potters often produce unique shapes with interesting texture and color, which themselves inspire creative modern arrangement.

TRADITIONAL STYLES INTERPRETED

LINE ARRANGEMENTS

Line arrangements, so beautifully executed by the Japanese, have become a medium of modern expression. Line is still the dominant and compelling feature, but dignified classic balance and proportions may now be almost precarious, and stately rhythms are sometimes shocking. When linear material is used to establish lines, it is selected for its beauty or uniqueness. Bare branches, fasciated or gracefully curving, or glycerine-treated branches of foliage are two possible choices. It is usually necessary to prune out distracting twigs and leaves to achieve clarity of line.

Figure 29. A modern line arrangement, by Mrs. Myles H. Reynolds.

Vines, peeled or natural, are used for their natural form or may be manipulated into fascinating twisting or spiraling shapes. Combinations of various materials and containers can be appraised, and different directions, proportions and means of obtaining balance can be judged.

Linear compositions generally have an open silhouette. Rhythmic movement of the lines may be sweeping or quick. Balance is generally asymmetrical, and off-center balance is often employed in the modern style. Material is kept to a minimum.

Line arrangements in stylized form may be composed by placing shapes, colors and textures to form a rhythmic path the eye can easily follow.

This arrangement illustrates the importance of line in an open silhouette with asymmetrical balance.

The rhythmic flow in an elliptical orbit is carried by the planes of the leaves on the sweeping branch and is completed by the planes of the flowers. The diagonal movement of the branch to one side is balanced by the bright yellow rudbeckia flowers. The brown glycerine-treated foliage was pruned to achieve clarity, grace and fluidity. The old earth-colored clay jug is well related to the design.

The line arrangement in *Plate 22* with strong vertical lines of stark simplicity and interest centered high in the design is composed of rough-textured red sumac, emphasized by the sheen of the glycerine-treated magnolia leaves. Gray-brown bark serves in lieu of a container.

MASS ARRANGEMENTS

This type stems from the European bouquet of the various historical periods and is traditional or modern in feeling according to the intent of the arranger and the choice of material. Step-by-step construction of a mass arrangement is shown under "Creating the Styles with Dried Flowers."

Plate 23 illustrates how an arrangement, although composed in the style of a definite historical period—in this case Victorian—is not typical of the period but is a modern interpretation. The colors chosen would not have appealed to the Victorian taste, but appear enticing to the modern eye. The design was created for a table in an office suite. Flowers used are: azalea, dahlia, stock, miniature gladiola, peony, sweet William, zinnia, celosia, lilac, delphinium buds, love-in-a-mist, orange blossom, lily-of-the-valley, *Viburnum carlcephalum*, lily, iris, pearly everlasting, hollyhock, tulip, rose and hydrangea. The foliage is dark brown *Ilex glabra* preserved by the glycerine method. The colors of some of the flowers which are so effectively used in this color scheme could be considered a dismal failure when removed from sand after they are dried; for example, the white lilac became tipped with brown, the white miniature pompom dahlias turned to beige. The soft beige color of the pearly everlasting and love-in-a-mist is acquired over a period of time. The beige of the small zinnias, iris and roses occurs from the fading of yellows upon exposure to light.

In *Plate 24*, a monochromatic color scheme shows the advantageous use of natural colors, as well as the new exotic colors sometimes attained in the preservation processes. (Information on color changes is given in Part Three and under "Color Changes.") The copper colors of the blueberry foliage and tropicana roses are newly acquired. Dahlias, nandina berries, and strawflowers possess their natural colors, and the celosia colors are faded.

Figure 30. Parchment color magnolia blossoms are beautiful with their own brown glycerine-treated foliage.

Figure 31. The elegant silver epergne of classic revival style holds flowers that repeat the colors of the exquisite needlepoint on the dining table chairs. An appropriate arrangement for a room of mixed period furnishing.

Figure 32. Red, white and blue anemone are a striking color accent, just the sort of thing decorators favor.

Figure. 33. A bouquet of colorful garden roses is appropriate for any decor.

MASSED-LINE

This type is an original American development that came into popular use in the 1930s. It combines the Japanese line with the European mass and may have a traditional or modern look.

Line provides the basic structure while a light mass develops the focal area and provides depth.

In *Plate 25*, an old-fashioned, sentimental look takes off in a new direction. The diagonal line is formed by gracefully curving trumpet vine

Figure 34. An example of the rhythmic Hogarth curve that has been extensively used.

lightly massed at the center with pink roses, blue delphinium, and blue and white love-in-a-mist. The airy baby's breath expands and carries the movement. A Bennington Parian ware vase adds to the feeling of delicacy and fragility.

Figure 35. Globe thistle with self foliage in a contrived design of "Early Garden Club" style.

Figure 36. A Massed-line type interestingly handled as a modern interpretation. Fasciated sumac and driftwood establish the line, while glycerine treated leather-leaf viburnum help to develop the vertical movement. Seed heads of *Allium aflatunense* and the larger *Allium albopilosum* contribute to the Mass. The container is modern Japanese stoneware. Designer, Mrs. Benjamin S. Killmaster.

NEW TRENDS IN ARTISTIC DESIGN

Modern, Free Style and Abstract styles are often exciting in their presentation of new concepts. The break with tradition is brought about by the use of different materials, through an awareness of the beauty of shapes, textures and colors that were previously considered inappropriate or even "ugly." Possibilities in their use is developed through experimentation and knowledgeable disregard of established principles. New notions in the use of proportions, scale and dynamic balance have brought new rhythms in space. Simplicity and clarity, and limitation in the use of material contribute to the development of three-dimensional designs in the new idiom.

MODERN STYLE

This style has a closer relationship to natural growth than free style or abstract.

In *Plate 26*, a clear definition of vertical and horizontal lines is made. The vertical column of the stoneware container is continued with the tall, straight stem of butterfly weed. The weathered wood accentuates the jutting horizontal line of the container, and is repeated once again by the old weathered chestnut board base. The orange lily brings it all into focus.

Figure 37. A sharply delineated contrast of shapes and lines using unrelated materials. The radiating pattern of the *Allium schubertti* held high on its straight stem is counterbalanced by the exotic round flower and leaf planes of the magnolia. The emphatic wisteria vine bisects the space between them and flows over the lip of the taller container and down to unify the design. Twin modern Japanese containers contribute to the interest. Designer, Mrs. Benjamin S. Killmaster.

Figure 38. The stark, heavy vertical line is broken with exploding interest high in the design. An auxiliary lighter, curving line carries the eye back to the base which is anchored by the *Allium giganteum* blossom. Designer, Mrs. Myles H. Reynolds.

Figure 39. The positive lines of the gun-metal containers are accentuated by the stained and polished driftwood, while glycerine-treated beech foliage lightens the bold form. Roses heighten interest in the focal area. Designer, Mrs. Benjamin S. Killmaster.

FREE STYLE

In this style a break from naturalism is apparent. Some materials are placed naturally and some unnaturally.

Plate 27 illustrates the dramatic use of selected forms found in nature. Roses provide another point of interest.

Figure 40. The horizontal branch of treated Julianna barberry is balanced by the two roses placed vertically in the uniquely shaped ceramic container. Designer, Mrs. Myles H. Reynolds.

Figure 41. One sees the strong line of the weathered wood swell up and away. The large crested celosia and contorted leaves, preserved by evaporation, are the stabilizing factor. The handsome container, important in the design, is made of clay from Mount Rainier—a flower arranger's treasure brought home from a trip to the West.

ABSTRACT

There are many degrees of abstraction. In the broadest sense, abstract applies to all non-representational work. In flower arrangement, when there is little or no relationship to natural growth the design becomes semi or completely abstract.

In the abstract design seen in *Plate 28*, the silver-gray weathered wood forms a strong geometric pattern sharply delineating solids and voids. The clusters of orchid rhododendron flowers contribute accents of shapes and color.

Figure 42. Black-painted, contorted roots of Australian pine, from Sanibel Island, Florida, outline an interesting spatial area. Pink peonies emphasize the high and low points of this abstract design. Designer, Mrs. Myles H. Reynolds.

ASSEMBLAGE

The classification "Assemblage" stems from a mid-twentieth-century art trend. It is created imaginatively of diverse elements which may or may not be fastened together.

Figure 43. A distinctive modern drama in black and white, the epitome of contrast! Opposing horizontal, vertical and round forms create a bold design. Designer, Mrs. James W. Griswold.

EXPRESSIVE

Expressive arrangements are used to interpret a theme, an idea or a mood, and can be expressed in the modern vernacular or traditionally. This type often appears in flower show exhibits.

Figure 44. This flower picture was used as a Garden Club Horticultural Exhibit. A bouquet of the Rosaceae family: roses and rose foliage, *Geum chiloense, Aronia arbutifolia, Malus coronaria, Spiraea bumalda* (Anthony Waterer). Designed "in the manner of" Jean-Baptiste Monnoyer by Mrs. Robert W. Wheat.

2 Creating the Styles With Dried Flowers

An array of astonishingly beautiful dried flowers makes possible the stimulating and fulfilling adventure of creating arrangements of any style to suit the most discriminating taste. One can be justly pleased and proud to survey an accumulation of exceptional dried material—the result of one's own skilled work. Detailed methods, techniques and procedures that make possible this accomplishment will be given under "The Art and Techniques of Flower Preservation."

Not only is there pleasure to be derived from creating dried flower arrangements as an artistic expression, but also in using them as decorations in the home and also in museums, historic houses and office suites.

Dried flower arrangements are valuable decorative art pieces that can be enjoyed and admired for a long time. To be beautiful they must be designed to express an idea, an emotion or a mood. The desired effect may be one of elegance, sophisticated modernity or casual charm.

Because they are made of real flowers, dried arrangements cannot be expected to be permanent decorative pieces. It is a pleasure and convenience to use them during the winter months, and with care their life can be extended. However, when they are no longer beautiful, they have lost their excuse for being. Exposure to humidity can cause certain flowers to collapse and lose their color, or perhaps they may be accidentally damaged. When critically appraised after long use they may just look "tired" and unattractive and should be discarded. Some material can be saved, reconditioned and used in new styles. (See "Grooming and Cosmetics.")

The flower arranger is anxious and happy to create new arrangements for the pleasure of the doing, as well as to provide a new and different decoration. It is always more interesting to have several arrangements on hand to be used interchangeably or to be moved about. The challenge of using distinctive dried flowers and foliage to exhibit their many possibilities is itself exhilarating.

For best colorful effect, dried flower arrangements must have good lighting. Some flowers lose their silken sheen during the drying process because textures are changed and reflect light only dimly. Light brings out the color to excellent advantage in their setting.

The setting determines the style, color and mood of an arrangement. Each should be a personal expression, suitable to the decor. A formal period room is enhanced by an arrangement created "in the spirit of" the period. Elegant flowers of fine texture, a well-chosen container, and a harmonious color scheme or related color accent are lovely. In a modern room, bold forms, intriguing lines, interesting textures, an imaginative container, a subtle or extravagant use of color are appropriate. In contemporary rooms, styles of furnishings are often mixed providing more leeway for different types of designs as suitable for the setting.

The size and sometimes the direction of the arrangement is determined by the space it is to occupy. The three-dimensional structure will be bound by the actual concrete lines of a niche or the limits set by a piece of furniture or the background space—real or imaginary. The scale of the material and the proportions of the design should be in good relationship to the entire room as well as the immediate surroundings.

Styles of artistic flower design today range from the traditional to the abstract.

As has been mentioned, traditional styles may reflect or be reminiscent of a definite period or historical style, or may be modern in feeling according to the intent of the arranger and the kind of material selected. There are three main types: line, mass and massed-line. Essentially the designs are geometric and may be in the shape of a triangle, rectangle, crescent, Hogarth curve, or a vertical or horizontal oval.

The latest contemporary styles are original and creative designs that depart from tradition. Three kinds are popular: modern, free style and abstract. Modern designs suggest a relationship to natural growth. Free-style designs depart from established principles and are not totally hampered by naturalism. In abstract design, natural materials are used with no relationship to anything that grows, but only as design elements.

Possibilities of Material

Once the purpose for which the arrangement is to be made and the limits of space for its placement are determined, the possibilities of various containers and kinds of materials at hand should be evaluated. They must be suitable in scale, color, texture, shape and pattern. The eventual choice will be those flowers and foliage ascertained as best to express the idea in mind.

It is always stimulating to choose the most perfect flowers and foliage, the most inspiring colors, the most intriguing lines and forms. Grooming and cosmetics treatment required will present each flower at its best. (See "Grooming and Cosmetics.") It is wise to discard any flowers that may have been damaged during storage.

Colorful flowers dried by the sand, silica gel and air-drying methods possess their own characteristics of beauty to spark the imagination. Parts Two and Three of this book list the methods best suited to achieve the most perfectly preserved natural form for each flower or piece of foliage and the desired or expected color. Naturally dried plant material, a gift of nature, becomes unique and inspiring when seen as elements for modern design. These two kinds of material can be combined with wonderful effect.

The choice of foliage contributes so much to the charm of the design. The greens brought in give a fresh look. Tendrils and fine-cut leaves give airiness and delicacy. Smooth or velvety textures may give the contrast needed. Branches of foliage in various shades of copper, bronze, brown and gray provide the desired line or background material for many kinds of arrangements.

The selection of material for arrangements of each style and type presupposes the intent of the arranger. However, materials themselves may inspire a design.

In any event, flowers and foliage selected for a mass generally possess different characteristics from those chosen for a line, and those for a free style would differ even more widely. Massed-line types incorporate flowers and foliage of many kinds.

Traditional styles become modern in feeling through a modern view-point in the selection of materials. *Plate 23* illustrates how an arrangement "in the Victorian manner" becomes a contemporary design in beige and brown. The Victorian taste in the use of color would have found this arrangement unacceptable and probably "ugly."

The flower arranger finds his materials already present in nature—line, form, pattern, texture and color. He need not create these elements of design but see them imaginatively. A rose is not only a rose but a geometric shape, aflame with color. A branch is a line in motion, a living rhythm. Queen Anne's lace is a radiating pattern. Mullein leaves are velvety texture. Color and texture modifies all, and sensitivity to color makes it the most stimulating element of design.

COLOR

Dried flowers can be richly colorful for many natural hues are captured and strikingly unusual colors also result. A full range of color, or at least favorite colors, should be available for desired effects.

Color has three qualities or dimensions: hue, value and chroma. Hue is almost synonymous with color, and value is the lightness or darkness of a hue. Light values are loosely referred to as tints and are light in weight, while dark values, called shades, are heavy. Chroma refers to the intensity or strength of a hue. Tones are grayed values, and neutral colors are those which are so greatly reduced in value and chroma that they possess no identifiable spectrum color.

Colors are spoken of as being warm or cool. Green, blue and violet are cool, and red, orange and yellow are warm. They also possess the quality of advancing or receding. Warm colors advance and cool colors recede.

In composing color harmonies, teachers and students find a twelve-hue color wheel valuable. This type incorporates hue, value and chroma of six standard and six tertiary colors.

The most appealing combinations of color fall into two categories; related and contrasting. Monochromatic and analogous are related harmonies. Contrasts result from hues that lie opposite on the color wheel. There are modifications of opposition: split complements, triads, double-split complements, tetrads and still others more complicated.

In monochromatic color schemes—using only one hue—contrasts in light and dark values and varied textures and forms gives interest to the arrangement.

Analogous color schemes lie next to each other or are neighboring hues on the color wheel but employ only one primary color. Two favorite combinations are green-yellow, yellow, orange-yellow, orange (warm); and violet-red, violet, violet-blue, blue (cool).

Complementary color schemes are strong contrasts. Red and green, a favorite at Christmas, and yellow and violet, the Easter colors, are direct complements and demonstrate this vitality.

A split complement consists of one color with the two colors that adjoin its complement on the color wheel. It is one of the best and easiest of color schemes, being more subtle than direct complements.

The triad has been well used by many noted artists. It is often skillfully employed in interior decoration, being a comfortable yet an interesting scheme.

The color wheel can be employed to work out further combinations, and all have infinite possibilities through the use of different intensities and values.

Color harmonies can be mediocre or disturbing if carelessly used, and superbly enjoyable if used well. If one does not have a good color sense, study can bring greater pleasure in its use.

In flower arrangement, balance, dominance, contrast, rhythm, scale and proportion are as applicable to color as to other design elements.

Good color balance depends on the distribution of visual weight. A small area of brilliant color will balance a large area of neutralized color.

Stability is easily gained by placing dark colors low and light colors high and on the edges, or by placing bright colors low and weak colors high and on the edges.

In each harmony one color should be dominant. Rhythms are gained through gradation in value and intensity and sequence of hues. Unequal scale and proportions prevent monotony, and contrasts are vitalizing.

CONTAINERS

A well-chosen collection of good containers cannot be overemphasized. The right container is a necessary element in any composition. Some designs are marred by poor containers, which is inexplicable for so many excellent choices are available. Good reproductions of classic vases of all shapes and styles can be collected and, hopefully, some beautiful antique pieces as well. Many containers of contemporary styles made of pottery, porcelain, glass, wood and metal are of exceptional quality and handsome shapes. Potters are producing excellent and imaginative work. Baskets and household utensils can also be used imaginatively. Containers may also be improvised—a piece of wood, a shell, a rock, building materials, or industrial gadgets. The supply is as unlimited as the imagination.

The container, as an intrinsic part of the design, must contribute to it and be related in size, shape, color and texture. It may be emphasized or minimized in importance. A container may be so stimulating that it influences the choice of all other materials and remains dominant in the design.

SUPPLIES

Devices for holding flower stems and wires, branches and wood securely in the desired position are required. These include floral foam, Styrofoam, pin-point holders, tape, wedges, wire and lead strips.

Floral foam is sold under such trade names as Quickee, Oasis and many more. Florists often use it, soaked with water, to hold fresh flowers in place. Of course, it is used dry for dried flowers. It is available in small cylinders and bricks from which pieces can be shaped to fit the container for it is easily cut with a knife.

Pin-point holders provide a good means of support for heavy material. It is sometimes necessary to anchor them with floral clay.

Natural stems, both hollow and sturdy, are needed to extend stem length and camouflage wires. Hopefully, an adequate supply of hollow stems is on hand. Long stems of air-dried flowers, such as Prince's feather celosia and globe amaranth, can be utilized. Stems of such flowers as day lilies and larkspur, which are hollow, should have been picked as soon as the flowers were spent and laid to dry in a dark dry place. Sturdy stems, such as those of air-dried goldenrod, are useful to support heavier flowers in an arrangement. Stems of glycerine-treated foliage to which large blossoms, such as magnolia, can be wired are attractive.

Wire is also useful to extend stem length—24-gauge for the smaller flowers, and 20-gauge for the heavier kinds. (See "Wiring to Strengthen and Lengthen Stems.")

Chain-nosed wire cutters of the mechanic's pliers type are useful not only for cutting wires but as forceps to place and extract flowers in arrangements.

Shears or clippers are needed to cut stems neatly.

Good tools are necessary for good work.

Floral tape in green and brown colors is used to cover wires and bind together added wires and stems to increase the stem length.

Tape is required to fasten floral foam into the container so that it will not become dislodged. This may be the florist's Davee tape, adhesive tape or strapping tape.

White glue, which dries transparent, may be needed for replacing dropped petals.

Supplies may be purchased at the florists, hardware stores and specialty shops.

MECHANICS

The arrangement of dried flowers involves a different technique in the control of mechanics than that for fresh flowers.

For abstract and free style, and sometimes modern designs, dried flowers are advantageous because no thought must be given to providing sufficient water to keep fresh flowers in odd positions in good condition. It is a simple matter to wire dried flowers in any desired position. This was done to fasten the rhododendron blossoms seen in *Plate 28*, and the peonies in the abstract design, Figure 42.

Pin-point holders are used to support sturdy stems, driftwood, branches, palm spathes, roots, vines and similar material. It is advisable to slash the ends so that they can be more easily impaled on the pins. Sometimes a specially designed pin-point holder is useful—one that has a screw at the back. To hold material that cannot be forced into a pin-point holder, the screw is screwed into the wood and the pins are locked into another larger pin-point holder that serves as the basic holder. It is sometimes advisable to anchor pin-point holders with floral clay.

Wedges, tape, wire, floral clay, lead strips and Styrofoam may also be used to hold material in the desired position.

Floral foam has many qualities that make it an excellent choice for the support of stems and wire for mass and massed-line, and some line arrangements. Wires and dried stems can be placed without difficulty and are held firmly. It is helpful to find that it is even possible to insert delicate natural stems without breaking. This is not possible when using Styrofoam.

Floral foam is easily shaped to fit snugly into containers for it can be cut with a knife with no difficulty. The bottom part of tall vases is filled with pieces of foam. If additional weight is desired, sand is used instead. (If sand alone is used, the position of the flowers is likely to shift, which spoils the design.) The top piece of floral foam should extend about an inch above the rim of the container. This provides a larger area and stems can be easily inserted from all directions. When using tall glass containers, foam is fitted only into the top part. Foam should be placed carefully for excessive pressure will crush it and destroy its capacity to hold stems firmly.

A narrow strip of tape, either adhesive tape, strapping tape or Davee tape, placed across the foam and fastened over the rim of the container will keep it from becoming dislodged. Two strips at right angles will hold a block of foam securely in a wide-mouthed bowl or flat container. Tape may be split lengthwise to make it about $1/8$ to $1/4$ inch in width, which is adequate. Figure 45 shows a tall container prepared and ready for the next step.

Flowers and foliage on their natural stems have an attractive appearance. Flowers that have had wires substituted for their stems when dried in a face-up position require some treatment to camouflage the wires where they will be visible in the arrangement. This can be done by using an attractive dried stem that approximates the natural stem in size, texture and color. One technique is to slip the wire through a required length of hollow stem so that it protrudes at the bottom and fasten the two together at this point with floral tape.

Prince's feather celosia stems of all sizes are extraordinarily useful because they have a spongy inner substance that holds both wires and natural stems firmly. The smaller stems provide excellent means of extending the length of short-stemmed flowers, such as separated clusters of hydrangea. Their short stems can be held and inserted with chain-nosed wire cutters. (Other methods risk the danger of breaking the petals.) These celosia stems may also be used to camouflage wires, and at the same time extend stem length. The wire of wired flowers can simply be inserted down into the spongy substance to anchor it firmly. A chain-nosed wire cutter is also an excellent tool for this operation. This same technique can also be used for long, hollow stems, but perhaps a drop of glue will be required at the top to hold the flower in place.

Sturdy stems, such as those of goldenrod, are useful to extend stem lengths of the heavier flowers because they can be anchored more securely in the floral foam and will support the flower in good position. A 24-gauge wire is adequate for small flowers, and 20-gauge for medium sizes. Wires and stems are easily bound together with floral tape to increase their length. Floral tape may be used to cover that portion of the wire visible in the arrangement. The technique for wrapping involves taking a length of tape from the roll, then wrapping one lap around the wire and squeezing to fasten it tightly. Twirl the wire with the thumb and index finger of one hand while pulling and smoothing the tape down the wire with the other. It is not necessary to wrap the entire length; in fact, bare wires are more easily controlled when inserting into the foam.

Stems and wires should not be placed deeply into the foam. Except for heavy flowers, less than an inch is sufficient. Better control of the position of the flower head can be gained in this manner, and more stems and wires can be placed without interfering with each other. This is particularly important when working with a narrow-mouthed vase.

COMPOSITION

The approach to composition is discussed in a most interesting way by Dorothy W. Riester in her book, *Design for Flower Arrangers.*

> Design is the orderly fitting together of visual experiences into an integrated, expressive form. Since design is not a product but a *doing process*, an activity, each designer must arrive at his own design structure. There is no preplanned, correct, compositional structure on which to hang the parts of a design. The way you fit together visual experiences is what creates the structure, but this need not be, and indeed cannot be, by a lone uncharted path of trial and error. We are individuals living in a present culture and we are inheritors of a cultural past. As designers, we are accompanied by a host of fellow artists, those of today and also those who have gone before us.

Study the work of the great artists—in various fields of art. Their experience will become your experience. We would be foolish, indeed, if we did not utilize the knowledge of the past and share in the present expression. Every artist has had his master: El Greco learned from Tintoretto, Goya from David, Cézanne from Poussin. Roualt wisely queries, "Have you ever seen anyone born by his own unaided efforts?"

Study the compositional methods and techniques of many artists. Experiment, use the discovered methods in your designs. Make the experience your own and then go on and use it to express your own intent. Mimicry can never create a living, vital art. Growth demands restatement and change.

Both the experienced arranger and newcomers to the art of flower arrangement find dried material offers a wonderful opportunity to explore, practice and acquire proficiency.

Composition is the means of making a work beautiful, and consciously or unconsciously, the principles of design are employed—balance, dominance, contrast, rhythm, proportion and scale.

Balance may be achieved symmetrically as in most of the traditional styles of Europe, and asymmetrically as in classic Japanese style. Off-center balance is frequently employed in contemporary styles.

Dominance is a unifying key to establish order. One aspect—one color, one texture, one line—must be emphasized while others play a subordinate role.

Contrast gives variety and vitality to the design.

Rhythm is the movement that directs the attention and organizes the elements in pleasing relationship.

Proportion deals with areas and relative amounts—to the size relationship between one part of the arrangement and another, and to the space it occupies.

Scale deals with parts and relative sizes. It pertains to the size relationship of component parts of the arrangement.

As has been noted, mass arrangements were masterfully composed by the flower painters of various schools in Europe. They exhibit a love of flowers and an appreciation of their marvelous colors and infinite variation in form.

Design and Construction of Mass Arrangements

This type is made today to catch the spirit of a definite historical period or the work of a particular artist. Arrangements are also composed in an altogether fresh interpretation of this three-dimensional, geometric, closed form.

Dried flowers are most valuable for mass arrangements for use during the winter months when flowers from the garden are not available.

The profusion of flowers required for a mixed arrangement should have been preserved in a variety of kinds and sizes with certain requirements in mind. Three categories of flowers and foliage are needed to provide essential forms for many styles—rounded, elongated and transitional.

Rounded-form flowers are center-of-interest types for they attract and hold the attention. Included are such flowers as roses, lilies, crested celosia, zinnias, tulips, marigolds, carnations, peonies, dahlias, camellias and daisies. A variety of colors and sizes is important. Leaves, such as magnolia, pachysandra, cecropia, hollyhock, ivy and galax, are useful as round forms or planes.

Elongated forms, such as long slender spikes, give airiness to the silhouette and may be used to establish the height, width and depth of the arrangement. They may be straight or curved and include delphinium, larkspur, grasses, grains, Christmas fern and fronds of maidenhair fern.

Elongated spray forms, such as goldenrod, dock, lilac, deutzia, nandina berries, butterfly weed and Prince's feather celosia, and foliage—crab apple, mountain laurel, forsythia, peony, rose, beech and blueberry—are valuable. They provide volume and gradation between the spikes and the round.

Transitional materials are spray or cluster types that serve in dried arrangements as "filler" material to provide density at the center. Clusters of hydrangea are excellent for this use. Pearly everlasting and sprays of foliage and goldenrod are also used in this way.

Small flowers and foliage of unusual form contribute vitality to arrangements through contrast. Variety and interest is provided by feverfew, columbine, globe amaranth, small strawflowers, acroclinium, pansies, love-in-a-mist, small daffodils, globe thistle, butterfly weed, grape tendrils, trumpet vine and grasses.

Compatibility of foliage and flowers must be considered because in most cases foliage is preserved separately.

Innumerable variations are attainable in mass type arrangements. They may be stylized or casual, imposing or dainty, flamboyant or serene, compact or airy, rounded or pyramidal, tall or low, colorful or muted.

Flowers, foliage and container are selected with one aim in mind— their effectiveness for the style, shape, color and size of the arrangement in relation to its placement in the setting.

Flowers are composed to establish a three-dimensional structure of interesting silhouette. Within the outline, material is placed to create areas of interest and definite patterns. In an arrangement with a triangular silhouette, a triangular pattern can be repeated within the outline. In a round or oval type, curved lines create the rhythmic paths. Vitality in movement is achieved by balance counter-balance of these areas in an overall symmetry. Rhythm is attained through repetition, radiation and gradation. Studied gradation in size, shape, color and texture are employed for a smooth flow of the rhythm between the centers of interest.

One selected color should be dominant. The main center of interest should have special emphasis, showing the brightest colors and possibly the greatest value contrast.

Rhythm in color is obtained by a related movement through gradation in values or intensity in the dominant color, or a sequence of colors as in an analogous color scheme.

Proportions should vary in amounts of different hues, values and intensity.

Step by step construction of a mass arrangement shows procedure for handling fragile dried material. This arrangement was inspired by an exhibit at the Chelsea Flower Show and was created as a personal interpretation of the Edwardian style.

Step 1 Preparation of the Container.

In Step 1, the tall, slender Sheffield vase is chosen because it is right for the style, establishes the period and will properly become an integral part of the design. Sand filled the lower volume of the vase for weight, then a round of floral foam was shaped, fitted snugly into the top third to rest on the sand base and fastened securely with tape. It extends above the rim of the container to provide additional surface into which stems can be inserted from any direction.

Figure 45.
Step 1—Preparation of the container.

Step 2   Building the Outline.

In Step 2, flowers and foliage were selected to be in good relationship to the container in scale, color and texture, and to the style in mood. The size and shape of the arrangement was established in relation to the size and shape of the container and the imaginary space it would occupy.

A triangular silhouette was begun with the green Christmas fern. The height and width is in proportion to the slender volume of the container, being twice as tall and one and one-half times as wide. These directional lines were reinforced and repeated with plumes of goldenrod. All were spaced to radiate from the center forming an interesting pattern of solids and voids. The elongated and curving forms of both the fern and the goldenrod become less dense until they become semi-airy and then airy tips leading into space. This quality and the variation in lengths make an outline of graceful irregularity.

Symmetrical balance was obtained by extending the material with equal weight on all sides of the central axis: top, sides, back, middle ground and down. The ivy and rose foliage swoop out and curve downward in the direction characteristic of the Edwardian style.

The use of a turntable facilitates turning the arrangement for critical appraisal from all sides.

Figure 46.
Step 2—Building the outline.

Step 3 Providing Density.

In Step 3, hydrangeas of muted beige and copper shades were selected to provide density low in the center of the arrangement. This is necessary because the eye does not like to see through a mass in this area. Hydrangea is one of the better flowers for this purpose because the rounded clusters of small petals have a diffusive quality. (Material used to create density serves an additional purpose in dried flower arrangement—that of hiding wires, floral foam and other evidences of mechanics.) It is extended toward the outline in an irregular pattern to give a full-bodied but un-crowded look.

While building the basic form one should have in mind the approximate position of the larger rounded-form flowers. Sometimes it is advisable to place at least some of them temporarily to determine where they will fit best into the design so as to reserve space for them. These lovely, large flowers are fragile and easily broken when being handled and should not be permanently placed until the background is completed.

Figure 47.
Step 3—Providing density.

Step 4 Design Within the Outline.

In Step 4, tulips, dahlias and roses were placed to create areas of interest in rhythmic lines. Their gleaming copper colors and round form attract attention, carrying the color and sheen of the container throughout the design.

The tulip, off-center at the rim of the container, is on a plane to display the markings in its deep cup and directs the movement to swing to the next tulips higher in the design. The off-white roses bring emphasis to the focal area because of their contrasting light value.

Depth was engendered by overlapping. The dahlias, particularly the darker ones, all being deeper in the mass, and the tulips and roses advancing so that the front of the arrangement is not flat. Turning of heads creates movement and a feeling of depth.

Spaces between flowers were varied by interesting intervals and without crowding. Each flower should have nodding room and be self-supporting.

Figure 48.
Step 4—Design within
the outline.

Step 5   Completing the Design.

Plate 19 shows how smaller flowers add variety and contrast while contributing to the smooth flow of the rhythmic movement through repetition and transition. Daffodils were used to repeat the off-white color, extend the lines of the roses and make an easy path leading through the arrangement. Butterfly weed is a pleasant change from density to the outline material. Native columbine adds variety and sprightliness to the outline, and nudges the directional flow of the rhythm. The little ranunculus exerts a surprising emphasis where it is needed. Strawflowers add to the burnished glow of the dominant copper color in the contrasting color harmony.

The completed form has a dominant, slender, triangular silhouette, with downward sweeping lines at the sides, reminiscent of the Edwardian style with repeating triangular rhythms.

Part Two

THE ART AND TECHNIQUES OF
FLOWER PRESERVATION

3 Understanding Dried Materials

Dried flowers can look fresh and real or fantastic and exotic. They
can be elegance itself with their own kind of beauty. They can have the
natural charm of simple field and garden flowers, or they can attain new
and intriguing colors to spark the imagination. Ever-increasing kinds of
plant material can be preserved with perfection of form and variety of
color through new methods in use by the amateur today and improvement
in techniques using methods long in use. Because dried flowers can be
truly beautiful, they are appropriate for flower arrangements of all styles
and can be used in good taste with much pleasure.

*Claim to
Distinction*

The best method of preservation should be found to produce the qualities desired for each flower. Because flowers differ so widely in structure,
substance, color and texture, different methods will be required for different kinds.

Many kinds of flowers can be attractive when preserved by the air-drying method. Some keep their natural form as well as their color and have
been appreciated and used since ancient times, earning the classification
"Everlastings." Clusters of very small flowers, such as baby's breath and
goldenrod, can also be air-dried with pleasing appearance, for although the
individual flower petals collapse, this is not readily apparent because of
their small size. However, with most flowers, shriveled and shrunken
petals and drooping and matted florets are disconcerting, even when the
beautiful color is retained.

The sand and silica gel methods of drying are recommended for excellence in the retention of color, and especially in the preservation of
the exquisite characteristic form which gives dried flowers their claim to
distinction. Many kinds have a more natural appearance when dried in
sand. Others have better substance and textural qualities when preserved
in silica gel.

Flowers should be crisp without looking stiff; petals should have a fresh, relaxed appearance with good texture and substance, never shrunken with burned petal edges, or thin and translucent. Each flower's characteristic structure should be perfection—not bent, broken or damaged with petals missing or dirty with a clinging residue.

Colors of dried flowers are a most exciting and delightful phenomenon. It is a joy to admire the lovely blues of delphinium; the pinks, whites and reds of peonies; the natural golden color of black-eyed Susans and the yellows and oranges of marigolds; the pleasingly muted or the strikingly vivid hues of roses; the jewel colors of verbenas and the whole gamut of values in the array of hues found in tulips. Most unusual are pink camellias that have acquired a band of moss-green color at the ruffled petal edges or white camellias with beige markings or magnolia blossoms that look like parchment.

Color Changes   The natural colors of many flowers can be retained, but many color changes can be expected to occur when flowers are dried. The actual nature of color in flowers is complex, and color is not fixed but modified as the chemistry of the tissues changes. The changes that occur on the living plant—when flowers come into bud, reach maturity and then fade—is often conspicuous. When flowers are dried these natural changes are even more pronounced, with an actual change in hue taking place in some cases. The most noticeable and numerous changes are those of the reds and pinks. Orange-reds turn to red; blue-reds have the blue accentuated, sometimes turning to purple. Clear pinks keep their true color, but rose-pinks, having the blue intensified, turn to lavender or even magenta, which is most disappointing if magenta is not a favorite color. Other color changes are mostly those of value—dark colors turn darker and light colors fade. Whites sometimes turn cream or beige. It is amazing, however, to find that orange zinnias turn to bright pink, and some reds turn purple. Greens exhibit little change during the drying process, but may fade upon exposure to light because the chlorophyll disintegrates. Rapid drying produces brighter colors and slower rates more muted shades and gradations. The rate of dehydration is rapid when the desiccant silica gel is used, and colors are bright and intensified. The rate is variable when the sand-drying method is used, so muted colors as well as bright colors can be produced. It is advisable to dry some kinds of flowers, especially roses, by both methods to obtain a choice of colors. Some fading of colors takes place when flowers are exposed to strong light over a period of time.

Preserved material is fragile and perishable when subjected to unfavorable conditions. Winter bouquets keep their beauty in the dry atmosphere of heated rooms. Air conditioning also provides a suitable atmosphere because moisture is removed from the air during the process. So today dried arrangements can be used as decorations during the summer, and the life of the winter bouquet is extended. A dehumidifier can turn any room into an ideal workroom and storeroom during seasons of the year when conditions of humidity are high. A relative humidity not exceeding 60 per cent is ideal and provides a most acceptable condition for all but the most perishable flowers. When the humidity exceeds this amount for only a few hours, many dried flowers will absorb moisture from the air back into the tissues so that crispness is lost, the petals and stems become limp, causing them to wilt and droop or even collapse. Dampness also causes colors to become faded and drab, as has been learned from unhappy personal experience. On several occasions in early autumn or late spring dried flower arrangements have been taken to be placed on exhibit in rooms that were neither heated nor air-conditioned. The weather was rainy resulting in extremely high conditions of humidity. Flowers prone to being unstable under these conditions were ruined.

Dried Flowers Must Be Kept Dry!

The everlastings and other air-dried material are the least susceptible to deterioration. Flowers that must be dried by the sand or silica gel methods are more prone to be ruined by exposure to dampness and must be protected from above-average conditions of humidity. It is interesting as well as important to note that flowers of the same variety exhibit differences, depending on the stage of development, horticultural perfection, covering medium and rate and degree of dehydration. Different varieties also exhibit varying degrees of stability.

Information concerning these characteristics is given in Part Three.

Individual flowers must be protected from exposure to dampness after they have been dried by careful storing before they are used to make arrangements. Careful storing keeps flowers as beautiful as they are when removed from the medium in which they are dried. The entire arrangement can also be placed in protective storage during periods when there is danger of exposure to dampness in a room with the humidity in excess of 60 per cent. (See "Storing.")

Flowers and foliage for drying can be selected from the garden, the fields or the wild, and from the florist. They should be at their peak of perfection, never overmature, and free from insect or other damage. Any imperfections in flowers are exaggerated when they are dried. Cutting spring and summer flowers for winter use only prolongs the blooming

Selection of Plant Material

season in the garden since annuals and perennials will have a longer season of bloom if not allowed to go to seed, and many flowering shrubs can be pruned to advantage during the blooming season.

Plant materials listed in Part Three are good choices for most have good form, texture, color, substance and stability when dry; some, however, are "temperamental" and must be carefully protected from moisture. The selection, of course, depends on the kinds and colors desired and those available.

Certain flowers cannot be preserved to be beautiful or stable; for example, those that bloom and are gone in a day, such as rose of Sharon and daylilies; neither poppies nor petunias have sufficient substance to be preserved; and phlox, platycodon, geraniums, pinks and azaleas are quite perishable. Such flowers as China asters and chrysanthemums are prone to shatter, while gaillardia and calendula appear translucent with thin textural quality.

There are, however, no hard and fast rules because different varieties of the same kind of flowers have different characteristics, so it is advisable to experiment with those at hand and to remember that excellent new hybrids are being introduced. Horticultural perfection often determines success in the drying process making the "blue-ribbon winner" the best selection. It is my hope that others will experiment with many kinds of plant material and will be successful with kinds that the author has found difficult or has not had an opportunity to preserve.

It is suggested that many shapes and sizes and kinds and colors of flowers and foliage be preserved. A dried mass arrangement requires at least three times as much material as would be required for a fresh arrangement. A large and varied supply of dried plant material is necessary for the flower arranger to be able to choose just the right form or color, whether creating an arrangement in the traditional or in the latest modern art form. One begins with the flowers of the spring bulbs and continues until frost harms the last rose.

Forms for mass arrangements should usually be of different shapes, sizes and patterns:

Round-form flowers of different conformation, such as full-blown roses, dahlias, daisies, marigolds and zinnias;

spike-form flowers, such as larkspur, delphinium, Prince's feather celosia and foliage or ferns;

transitional forms, such as rose buds, lilac, goldenrod;

dainty and interesting forms, such as feverfew, deutzia, and daffodils;

graceful delicate foliage and ferns, such as maidenhair fern, tips of trumpet vine or ivy;

filler material, such as hydrangea, foliage, ferns, pearly everlasting and boneset;

dramatic forms, such as lilies and tulips. Flowers of different sizes must be combined for interest and contrast.

Flower forms for modern arrangements have to meet the requirements of the designer. Bold forms, interesting textures, dramatic line material and color are important.

4 Modern Methods of Drying Flowers

How much more interesting any craft becomes when we learn something of the historical background of present-day work. In a remarkable book by P. Giovanni Battista Ferrari of Sienna published in Rome in 1638, entitled *Flora—ouero Cultura di Fiori*, we find reference to the sand-drying method for preserving flowers. Chapter II of this book is entitled "Dried and Fake Flowers Which Look Fresh and Real," and the following is a translation from this chapter:

Art and skill can keep alive and everlasting a thing as frail and deciduous as the flower. If you have a natural gift for keeping flowers vigorous and lasting, and, once cut from their root, which gives them life, make them seem alive and fresh again, learn a new method which is better than the embalming used by the Egyptians, and which has been used in Germany only for a few years.

Take a vase of terra cotta or copper, or any wood container. Fill it up half-way through with fine sand which has been sifted, and then fill it all the way with clear water. Mix sand and water with a rod or a wood spatula so that the mud, if there is any, may decompose and wash out. When the sand has settled, remove the muddy water. Repeat this procedure as many times as it is necessary until the water is clear. Remove the cleansed sand and put it out to dry in the sun for a long time. Now prepare a vase for each flower; this container has to be of proportionate size and can be of terra cotta or tin. Take a flower, fully bloomed, with no moisture on at all, with a stem as long as you wish; with the left hand put the flower gently in the vase, about two inches down from the edge, without letting it touch the vase at all (sides and bottom); with the right hand place the sand all around it until the stem is completely covered; then spread out and arrange the flower petals, and finally cover the flower with more of the same sand. The tulip requires special attention; the triangular bud which sticks out must be cut, so that the leaves may remain well attached to the stem. Place the vase thus prepared on a porch, where there is enough sunlight, for two or three months. After this period of time, remove the flower, which will be fresh-looking as if just picked, except that the fragrance will be gone. You will enjoy it out of season either alone or in a bouquet with other flowers.

Another method of preserving flowers is shorter and quicker. Dip the flower in a strong solution of water and various salts. This solution is called "crisulea." The flower will not be soft, but it looks real.

(NOTE—He does not explain what kind of salts they are. The stem of the word comes from the Greek *xpugos* which means "gold.")

Ferrari also tells in this chapter how to press flowers between sheets of paper under weights, much as is done today. Then he suggests making a "Volume of flowers" by gluing these dried flowers on paper and arranging them in a book "as does one, Andriano Spigellio." He also describes "the fine art used in Flanders"—the skill of reproducing flowers in silk (fake flowers). A most exciting book, it also includes information on gardening and forcing as well as flower arranging.

In America, the sand-drying method of flower preservation was described in an article in the December 1788 issue of the periodical, "The American Museum or Repository of Ancient and Modern Fugitive Pieces &c. Prose and Poetical," published by Mr. Mathew Carey of Philadelphia.

Method of preserving plants in their original shape and colours.

Wash a sufficient quantity of fine sand, so as perfectly to separate it from all other substances; dry it; pass it through a sieve, to clear it from any gross particles, which would not rise in the washing: take an earthen vessel of a proper size and form, for every plant and flower, when they are in a state of perfection, and in dry weather, and always with a convenient portion of the stalk: heat a little of the dry sand prepared as above, and lay it in the bottom of the vessel, so as equally to cover it; lay the plant or flower upon it, so that no parts of it may touch the sides of the vessel: sift or shake in more of the same sand by little and little upon it, so that the leaves may be extended by degrees, and without injury, till the plant or flower is covered about two inches thick; put the vessel into a stove, or hot house, heated by little and little to the 50th degree; let it stand there a day or two, or perhaps more, according to the thickness and succulence of the flower or plant: then gently shake out the sand, upon a sheet of paper, and take out the plant, which you will find in all its beauty, the shape as elegant, and the colour as vivid as when it grew.

Some flowers require certain little operations to preserve the adherence of their petals, particularly the tulip—with respect to which, it is necessary, before it is buried in the sand, to cut the triangular fruit which rises in the middle of the flower; for the petal will then remain more firmly attached to the stalk.

A *hortis siccus*, prepared in this manner, would be one of the most beautiful and useful curiosities that could be.

The sand-drying method is used today with great success and as much delight as in the seventeenth and eighteenth centuries, and the author has a personal preference for this method for most flowers.

Each flower must be surrounded and completely covered with sand to support it until the moisture evaporates and it will hold its natural shape. (See "Covering Techniques.")

Sand, being a fine, granular material, has the desired property of flowing freely to cover all parts of the flower uniformly with an even distribution of weight. This pressure on all surfaces supports the natural form of each petal during dehydration, and thus retains the beauty of the characteristic form.

ADVANTAGES OF THE SAND-DRYING METHOD

Sand is an inert material that has no reaction on or with the flower substance. Because of this quality the flowers are never excessively dehydrated and keep a natural appearance. Petals have a relaxed not a taut look about them, for some degree of flexibility is retained. There is no excessive shrinkage or brittleness, and petal edges are never burned. The necessity for specific timing and urgent removal is eliminated. The period of time required for drying varies from one to three weeks depending on the size, substance and compactness of the flower and the drying conditions. They may be removed from the sand at any convenient time. As a matter of fact, certain sprays of small flowers, such as feverfew, may be left in the sand until one wishes to use them. This prevents loss of the tiny petals which occurs if they become entangled. Broad-petaled flowers, such as full-blown roses, should be removed and stored when dry to prevent pitting of petal surfaces.

No residue is present when most flowers are dried by this method as sand does not cling to flower surfaces, with the exception of those with hairy or velvety textures. This proven ancient method is easy and cheap with few shortcomings.

A wide and fascinating range of colors can be obtained by the use of this method. Rapid drying in a very warm, dry place produces the brighter colors. Slower drying produces more muted shades.

Desirable Conditions for Sand-Drying

Drying flowers in sand requires a warm, dry place in an *open* box in order to allow for rapid evaporation of moisture. This method of drying cannot be used successfully in a cool or damp area, such as a basement. Colors will be drab, flowers will not dry well and may even mold. A workroom where humidity is controlled by a dehumidifier set at 60 per cent provides an excellent drying situation. Any room free from dampness is adequate. Flowers dried at room temperature will have good but not brilliant color.

An ideal place to dry flowers is in the attic during a period of dry, hot weather where the temperature may range from about 50 degrees at night to about 120 degrees during the day. Since the temperature of sand does not fluctuate as quickly as air temperature, most flowers will be dry in one to three weeks. Under such conditions colors will be clear and bright. Suitable temperature and humidity conditions for drying flowers in an attic can usually be had from mid-spring through the summer months, even though there is a great variation in weather. Colors will not be as clear and bright if the weather is cool or rainy; but then, variety of tones and shades of color are just the results one may wish to obtain. Relax and enjoy what nature and climate produce! When moving boxes filled with sand-covered flowers, it is imperative that they be carefully handled to prevent shifting, in which case the shape of the flowers may be ruined.

The kitchen oven of a gas stove with a burning pilot light provides an excellent place for drying. Four days to a week is adequate for many kinds. When the oven is needed for baking, set the box of flowers aside, then after the oven has cooled replace the box. The lowest setting of an electric oven has proven too hot so that flowers are likely to be "baked" with loss of color and substance. Bottom heat provided by hot water radiators or water heaters might be advantageous. The bottom of the box would require some insulation to prevent overheating.

Sand is not only pleasant to use but cheap and readily available. White sand, sold for children's sand boxes, is available for purchase at many stores. It does not require any special preparation as it is already dry, clean, fine-grained and free of foreign material. Fine, white silica sand, used in construction work, can be purchased from building-supply companies. Both kinds give excellent results. If one wishes to use sand from rivers, lakes, sand pits or the beach, it must first be thoroughly washed, dried and sifted to remove foreign matter and tiny pebbles. Because sand does not absorb moisture from the air or the flowers themselves, it can be reused without special treatment or preparation, although sifting is sometimes required to remove accumulated debris.

Sturdy cardboard boxes for sand-drying in a variety of sizes can be easily obtained—larger boxes for storing sand, and smaller ones for different shapes in which to cover flowers are needed. Remember that large boxes filled or even partially filled with sand become heavy and difficult to handle. The seams should be sealed with good-quality package sealing tape or masking tape to prevent sand from trickling out, which can be a real nuisance. Plastic or tin containers may also be useful, especially for individual flowers.

This is a new, popular, excellent and easy means of preservation for many kinds of flowers. Success is largely determined by rigid adherence to strict timing.

Silica Gel-Drying Method

Silica gel has been prepared in fine mesh for the special use of flower drying and is sold under such trade names as Flower-Dri, Flower Keep, etc. It is a form of colloidal silica possessing many fine pores, an extremely absorbent material that takes up moisture not only from flowers but from the air as well. This necessitates keeping it in an airtight container. Bright blue granules have been added which lose their color when the maximum moisture content is reached, at which time the silica gel should be dried in the oven at 250 degrees until the blue color returns. Seal the container to make it airtight, and the silica gel is ready for use again as soon as it cools.

Silica gel for flower drying has the appearance of very white sand but is much lighter in weight. It flows well to cover and support the natural form of flowers in the drying process.

After flowers are covered (see "Covering Techniques") the container in which they are placed must be closed tightly and sealed with masking tape or some similar tape to make it airtight. A label should indicate date, time and kind of flower. Then the container can be set aside in any convenient place until the flowers are dry. For removal, see "Uncovering Techniques." If flowers are not completely dry when removed from the silica gel, there is no problem for they can be placed carefully on top of a quantity of dry silica gel leaving them *uncovered*. However, if stems are not dry they should be re-covered. After the container is sealed and labeled, set aside for a few more days.

It would be helpful if the exact number of days and hours required could be definitely known. However, there are so many factors to be considered that the timing varies. First, this depends on the dryness of the silica gel since it can be used in some instances more than once before it must be put into the oven to be dried itself. So, naturally, the drier the silica gel the quicker the flowers will be dried. Flowers themselves dry at different rates according to their substance, size and compactness. For example, roses with thin petals will dry faster than those with thicker petals, and full-blown roses will dry faster than rose buds. Approximate timing is given for many flowers in Part Three, but it must be remembered that circumstances can make a difference.

ADVANTAGES OF THE SILICA GEL-DRYING METHOD

Kinds of flowers subject to broken petals and shattering have this calamitous possibility reduced. Those with dramatic shapes, such as lilies, tulips and iris, are more easily preserved by this method. Because silica gel is a lightweight substance, stress on the crisp petals is reduced during the uncovering process to release the flower without damage. Large blooms, such as magnolia and some dahlias, tend to lose petals or shatter completely when dried in sand but are preserved intact in silica gel.

Good, clear colors are attained because of rapid dehydration. Brightly colored flowers become vivid, and delicate pastel tints are retained.

Better substance, texture and stability results when *problem* flowers are rapidly dehydrated. Some kinds, such as daffodils, pansies, hyacinths, orchids and rhododendron, which have a thin translucent appearance when dried more slowly, attain a better texture and are less susceptible to damage from humidity when preserved by this method. These advantages are increased when the new quick "quick-drying" method is used.

NEW METHOD WITH SILICA GEL—QUICK "QUICK-DRYING"

Flowers can be even more rapidly dehydrated when covered with silica gel and dried in an *open* tin in the oven of a kitchen stove. The temperature setting should be the lowest possible—150–180 degrees. Timing is again not definite because of variation in oven controls and size, substance and compactness of flowers. Approximate time ranges from 8 to 12 hours for small, fragile flowers, such as bachelor's buttons and forget-me-nots; 12–18 hours for daffodils and pansies; 18–24 hours for lilies, tulips and peonies. For problem flowers, the best substance, texture and stability is obtained by the use of this method.

Silica gel is quickly available for reuse, and many flowers can be preserved during a short season of bloom when they are available at their peak of perfection.

LIMITATIONS OF THE SILICA GEL METHOD

Since silica gel is a drying agent, it is mandatory that flowers be removed as soon as they are dry and before they become excessively dehydrated. This causes excessive shrinkage, burned petal edges, and brittleness to the point of causing flowers to disintegrate.

Residue remains after flowers are removed and must be cleaned off thoroughly for two reasons: for good appearance, and because residue on flower surfaces will absorb moisture from the air causing the flower itself to become damp.

A new "sandblasting" method is recommended for removing residue from flower and stem surfaces. (See "Grooming and Cosmetics.")

Tins for drying and for storing silica gel. Tins of the kind often used for fruit cakes at Christmastime are excellent for drying and for storing silica gel when not in use. These may be used for drying flowers with lids in place and sealed or without lids by the quick "quick-drying" method suggested in this book. It should be remembered that lids should be sealed with tape to make the cans airtight when storing. Plastic containers with airtight lids are also useful, but of course not in the oven.

Although silica gel is expensive, it can be used over and over again for a number of years.

Other Drying Media

Borax is a colorless, crystalline, slightly alkaline substance that has been used as a drying material for the preservation of flowers since the Gold Rush days. Where quick dehydration is desired, the use of borax has been supplanted in popularity by the newer silica gel method. It is thought that better form, color, natural appearance and cleaner surfaces can be obtained by the methods noted above. It is pleasant to find agreement with this opinion in a letter from England. It was stated that many flowers had been preserved beautifully using both the sand and silica gel methods. Upon reading about the borax method, it was tried—but with disappointing results.

Experience with the above and many other drying media, such as perlite, kitty litter, cornmeal and grits-borax mixtures used by the amateur, suggest that these methods have no decided advantages as compared with sand and silica gel, and many disadvantages.

Air-Drying Method   Air-drying is the easiest and best method for preserving many kinds of flowers. As a general rule, flowers need only to have the leaves removed and to be hung upside down in a dry, dark place until the moisture content is evaporated and they are dry. Flowers dried by this method have been used throughout the ages. The Greeks used immortelles for their funeral wreaths, and mention is made of them in herbals of Roman, Medieval and Renaissance times. They were also popular in the eighteenth and nineteenth centuries.

Everlastings or immortelles can be easily and inexpensively grown in the garden. Many new hybrids are available, offering a wonderful variety and range of color. These flowers are stable and keep their beauty of form and color for several years. Some of the most popular are acroclinium, strawflowers, globe amaranth and statice.

Other garden flowers that can be dried best by this method are celosia, both crested and plume types, baby's breath, and globe thistle.

Herbs can also be hung to dry and tucked into an arrangement for the delight of their fragrance. Some are also attractive and can be used for their own characteristic form or color. Sweet cicely is a lovely airy material, and lavender can be useful for its blue-gray color and seed head as well as its fragrance.

Berries and seed pods should not be overlooked as they can be picked and hung to dry at various stages of development for differences of color, texture and shape.

Some ornamental grasses, such as fountain grass, quaking grass or ruby grass, provide graceful small spike forms of different colors.

Several kinds of wildflowers which can be air-dried are invaluable for creating some styles of mass arrangements. Favorites are many varieties of goldenrod, pearly everlasting and several of the bonesets and dock.

When picking wildflowers to air-dry, it is recommended that gloves be worn, as they will protect the hands from scratches and stains.

Stripping the foliage from the stems is not a particularly difficult task if it is done when each stem is picked.

The stage of development at which flowers are picked to be air-dried determines their success and usefulness. Since the various kinds behave differently, many must be picked while still in the bud stage or partially open as they will continue to open while drying; whereas, others must be picked when they are fully matured. It is also advisable to substitute wire for stems of a few kinds. This information for each flower is given in Part Three.

Procedure for Hanging Flowers to Dry

Leaves should be stripped from the stems so that flowers will dry more quickly. (This will also contribute toward a neater and cleaner workroom.) While holding the stem just below the flower, a long downward swipe with a gloved hand or paper towel will remove the leaves. The material is arranged in small bunches with the stems fastened together near the ends with a rubber band. Should the stems shrink, as is generally the case, the rubber band will also shrink and hold the bunch more securely than if tied with string. The flower heads or sprays can be separated by spreading them out in a fan shape so they will not be crowded together or tangled. With the heads down, the bunches are hung over a line, on a nail or coat hanger, in a dark, dry place until the moisture evaporates. An attic, open closet or workroom is a suitable area for drying. Avoid damp areas and poor air circulation.

Collecting Naturally Dried Plant Material

Dorothy W. Riester, in her book *Design for Flower Arrangers*, includes a chapter on "Materials of Flower Arranging." She writes: "Think arrangement in your seeing, not necessarily a particular arrangement, just arrangement—in the same way that a poet hears words as poetry and a sculptor sees light and shadow in terms of sculpture. If you develop the habit of constant mental selection, you will discover that you have never really seen before. What you once viewed as just a stone or shrub or flower, suddenly assumes a special character. Much of the joy of flower arranging lies in the discovery of the world about us."

She suggests that we get inspiration from those materials that appeal to us personally. Perhaps it is the line of a bare branch or the texture of the mullein or the pattern of a cone that is appealing. Perhaps it is the airy quality of grass or grain, or the form and color of a seed pod. A dried flower arranger will often have the instincts of a squirrel and store away many treasures from which can be chosen the necessary shape, texture or color for use when creating an arrangement.

Collectors find material everywhere. A trip to the seashore yields exciting pieces of driftwood. From the tropics comes much exotic, bold material for modern arrangements. A walk through one's own garden, the fields or woodlands provides cones, pods, branches and fungi, as well as grasses and seed heads.

Conservation of Wildflowers

For all lovers of flowers, the conservation of native plants is as much a responsibility and patriotic duty as it is to collect and preserve any early Americana. Since a plant that is abundant in one region may be rare in another and sparsely distributed in yet another, picking should be done with discretion based on knowledge. It is recognized that the "advance of civilization" is a greater threat to the survival of wild species than picking wildflowers for pleasure or transplanting them to home gardens. State laws regarding conservation of natural resources should be observed. Never pick flowers that are protected by state law or growing in public parks. A printed list of these plants may be secured from the various states, conservation and preservation societies, or garden clubs. Ask the permission of the owner before picking wildflowers in fields and woods. It is generally accepted that native material on conservation lists may be used if cut from one's own garden.

Methods for Preserving Foliage

Most of the foliage used in arrangements must be preserved separately. Preserved foliage provides the arranger with a great variety of shapes, sizes, textures and colors. Consideration of the types of designs one wishes to create will determine the selection of material as well as the method.

Glycerine Method

Glycerine, which was discovered in 1799, is widely used to preserve many kinds of foliage.

The characteristic form, texture and pliability of leaves is wonderfully retained when the glycerine solution is absorbed up through the stem into the leaf tissues. This treated material is long-lasting, not perishable, and may even improve in appearance and quality of substance over a period of several years. This is truly distinctive material and a favorite of many flower arrangers. It is useful for all styles of arrangements.

Color changes occur as absorption takes place. Various shades of greens, browns, beiges and grays to almost black are produced; however, greens usually turn to brown over a period of time. Some browns turn a beautiful bronze hue when placed in sunlight.

Many kinds of foliage can be successfully preserved by this method. It should be mature and in good condition for immature leaves and stems will wilt and droop. Only mature foliage will have good substance and stability. Branches of broadleaf evergreens, such as mountain laurel, Juliana barberry and magnolia, are exceptionally lovely. Needled evergreens, such as the yews, provide another form, texture and color.

Branches of deciduous trees and shrubs, such as beech, apple, flowering crab, forsythia and blueberry, are excellent. The season at which deciduous leaves are preserved will determine their color. Branches treated in mid-summer often produce dark green colors which turn to dark brown after a period of time. Those treated when the leaves just begin to show their autumn colors will yield beautiful shades of russet hues.

The leaves of some herbaceous perennials, such as peonies and lily-of-the-valley, can also be preserved.

Glycerine can be purchased at drug stores. Solution is made of one part glycerine and three parts warm water. Mix well. The solution can be reused, but strained if necessary to remove dirt or mold. Heat to boiling and let cool to tepid before using if mold is present.

Foliage to be preserved should be groomed by removing damaged leaves and dust or dirt. Wiping leaves with a damp cloth or paper towel should be sufficient, or leaves can be washed. Stem ends are crushed or two slashes are cut an inch or two long to provide greater exposed area for good absorption. Prepared stems are stood upright in a glass jar about three-fourths full of the glycerine solution. The sizes and heights of the jars will depend on the length of the branches or stems—one-half pint, pint or quart. As many stems or branches can be preserved in one jar as can be accommodated without crowding or crushing any leaves. Depth of solution should be maintained at a level to cover the cut or crushed area. As it is absorbed, additional solution should be added. The use of glass jars is convenient for checking levels. Stabilize the jars so that they will not tip over. The process of absorption of the solution into the leaves is visible since color changes occur as the tissues become saturated. When the solution has reached the upper leaves and color change has occurred in the entire leaf, the branch or stem should be removed and hung upside down in a dry, dark place. Then the treated material may be stored in boxes or plastic or paper bags, if desired.

Care must be taken so that branches are removed before they become oversaturated for the solution will ooze out on the underside of the leaves. This is untidy and unattractive. Should this happen, polish dry with a soft cloth or paper towel.

The time required for the process is variable—three days to three weeks or longer. The process should be watched closely. Check the underside of the leaves when in doubt to determine the degree of absorption. For no discernible reason, some branches will not absorb the glycerine solution and wilt. Discard this material and try again.

> NOTE: Branches of foliage, such as magnolia, may be arranged artistically and used as a decorative piece and enjoyed while they are absorbing the glycerine solution. A needlepoint holder may be employed to hold the branches in place. Remove the solution when the absorption process is complete.

Stems of periwinkle (*Vinca minor*) and mature stems of ivy can also be preserved by absorption through the stem. This method is preferable to the immersion method because it is more tidy. Pronounced color changes do not occur, necessitating a close check.

Do's and don'ts for success with the glycerine method: Do select mature foliage only. Do place prepared stems directly into the glycerine solution. Do *not* place stems in water before processing or treating in glycerine. Do place foliage in glycerine solution as quickly as possible. Do not allow leaves to wilt before treating. Do maintain level of solution to cover prepared part of stems. Do check progress of treatment. Do remove when leaves have changed color. Do not leave stems in the solution after absorption is complete.

> NOTE: Some material that can be air-dried, such as goldenrod, grasses and grains, can also be perserved in glycerine using the same method as for foliage. Color changes occur.

PRESSING METHOD

This is a very easy way to preserve individual leaves, small branches of foliage and many kinds of ferns. Although the contour is lost and the foliage is flat, the green color can be retained by this method as well as the lovely autumn colors of deciduous trees and shrubs, such as maple, sweet and sour gum, beech, blueberry and sumac. White poplar is attractive when the underside of the leaves have turned white with the top a useful gray-green.

Foliages selected should be kept fresh. When branches are cut the stems can be placed in water to prevent wilting. Groom by trimming off imperfect leaves. Oiling leaves before pressing makes them more pliable when dry and also gives them a sheen. A light coating of cooking oil can be applied with a paper towel or soft cloth by wiping both the top and under surfaces of the leaves. This also serves to remove any dust or dirt.

Unglazed paper, such as newsprint or old telephone books, is best for pressing. Place branches between several thicknesses of newspaper. Arrange leaves so that they do not overlap, or fit small layers of newspaper between overlapping leaves. Additional layers of paper and branches can be built up and then all covered with a cardboard before weighting down with heavy objects. This distributes the weight evenly. Another way: One layer of branches can be arranged between several thicknesses of newspaper and placed under a rug on the floor. Walking over these seems only to improve their appearance. Very small branches and individual leaves can be pressed between pages of old telephone books which should be weighted down.

Time required for drying: two to four weeks, depending on leaf substance and size.

When ferns are pressed, they should be placed to retain graceful curves.

Storing is not a problem as pressed material does not need to be removed until it is used.

Sand-Drying Method

The natural contour of leaves, vines, ferns and small branches of foliage can be retained by this method. This material is as fragile as flowers when dried, but most useful in arrangements. The form and color of the foliage of roses, peonies, delphinium, hollyhock, dogwood, ivy and trumpet vine are very attractive. Some ferns, particularly maidenhair and the florist's Baker's fern, can best be preserved by this method.

Techniques for covering is the same as that for the horizontal position used to cover flowers, except that several layers can be covered. Cover each piece completely before adding the next.

Evaporation Method

Leaves of many tropical plants often used as house plants and herbaceous plants, such as aspidistra, dracaena and hosta, can be dried by standing stems in shallow water, allowing the water to evaporate and the leaves to air-dry. These assume intriguing shapes and brown and beige hues of various shades. They are interesting in modern style arrangements. They are brittle and must be handled with care.

5 Step-by-Step Techniques for Sand and Silica Gel Methods

Techniques and skills employed in using the sand and silica gel methods for drying affect quality and beauty. There is nothing difficult involved, really, but properly preparing the material you have picked —with some help from the lessons of experience—will make all the difference. One easily takes steps to insure that flowers to be covered are in best condition. Wiring of certain stems may be necessary to reinforce and maintain them in usable and attractive condition. It may be necessary to substitute wire for natural stems to facilitate the covering of some kinds of flowers. Other treatments may be required before flowers are dried to insure good or successful results. It is imperative, for example, that a few flowers be glued before they are dried to prevent shattering. The position in which each flower is covered and the way in which the covering medium is applied are of utmost importance for retention of the natural structural form. Uncovering must be accomplished in such a way as to prevent breakage since dried flowers are crisp and fragile. Here are some "recipes" that have given me satisfying results.

Conditioning Material

Garden flowers can be cut and taken immediately to be covered in the drying medium before they wilt. They should be fresh and dry with no trace of dew or rain.

It is recommended that many kinds of flowers and foliages be conditioned or hardened off before being placed in the drying medium. Flower arrangers and horticulturists are aware that flowers assume their best form when turgid—the tissues filled with water. This does not affect the drying time or color, but assures excellence of form.

It is more pleasant—and not so exhausting—to cut flowers, allow them to condition, and then cover them to dry in a leisurely manner at a convenient time. This eliminates the necessity of frequent trips to the garden.

Turgidity or crispness causes the flower to hold its shape while being covered, therefore making it possible to more easily cover the flower with the drying medium without changing the position of a single petal. It is impossible to cover wilted flowers successfully.

Take a cutting basket filled with containers of warm water to the garden or field. Those flowers that are at their best stage for drying can be cut and their stems placed immediately in deep water. Woody and thick stems will absorb water more readily if two-inch long slashes are made at the end. The bark can also be peeled back to provide more surface for absorption of water. Let flowers stand for several hours or overnight, preferably in a dark, cool place.

Flowers that will open to the desired stage in a day or two can also be cut. In this way they can be protected from insect or spray damage or rainstorms. The form of the flower is often improved by this means.

Short stems can be placed in soft drink bottles full of warm water. The narrow neck keeps the bloom from becoming wet. They will be crisp and turgid and ready to be covered in a short time. Flowers with short stems will not stay as fresh as long as those with longer stems.

Reconditioning wilted flowers. If flowers have wilted, they can sometimes be reconditioned by recutting the stems on a slant with a sharp tool and placing them in hot water. Let the flower heads lean out from the container so that the steam does not flow up and envelop them. Allow to stand until the flower is revived. Flower stems may also be cut under water to implement absorption of water.

Transporting flowers. Many kinds of flowers, including dahlias, lilies and tulips, can be transported for great distances without injury if they are freshly cut, laid flat in a box, and covered so that a flow of air does not dry them, or sealed in a plastic bag. Wilting is not harmful, but instead will help prevent breakage. When the destination is reached, the stems should be recut and placed in warm water so that in a matter of hours the flowers will be turgid and fresh again. Of course, flowers may also be transported in containers filled with water so that they will not become wilted.

PLATE 13. The formal
elegance of this exuberant
mass, a transitional style of
the Federal period, America,
is extraordinarily appropriate
for its fine setting, the John
Quincy Adams State Drawing
Room, Diplomatic Reception
Rooms, Department of
State, Washington, D. C.
Arranged by Mrs. Jack
C. Fuson.

PLATE 14. The American
eagle motif on the Chinese
export bowl is found on
rare and important furnishings
of the Federal period in the
James Monroe Reception
Room at the Department
of State. The arrangement
reflects the analogous color
scheme of the room.

PLATE 15. The shape of the classic urn and the full, heavy mound of flowers suggest the Greek Revival period in America.

PLATE 16. Dark, rich red and bronze colors of the handsome American Empire urn are repeated by the foliage and some of the flowers in the heavy bouquet.

PLATE 17. The fanciful vase and the colorful mass with its sprightly outline reflect the Victorian taste of the Romantic period.

PLATE 18. A misty light mass after a flower painting by Odilon Redon in the Art Nouveau style.

PLATE 19. An interpretation of the Edwardian style. The composition of this arrangement is shown step-by-step under "Creating the Styles with Dried Flowers."

PLATE 20. An *Ichyo* line arrangement using *Corylus contorta* as the three main lines assisted by two red roses. The bronze usubata was designed by Meikoff Kasuya, the Head-master of the Ikenobo school. Designer, Mrs. Paul E. Todd.

PLATE 21. Japanese free-style design. Scotch broom, deutzia and a single camellia blossom of exotic color acquired in the drying process accentuate the color and shape of the handsome *Raku* container made by Jean Amos. Designer, Mrs. Paul E. Todd.

PLATE 22. Stark simplicity with interest high in the design and the choice of material make this line arrangement modern. Designer, Mrs. Myles H. Reynolds.

PLATE 24. Color changes and natural colors are combined effectively in this mass arrangement of contemporary style.

PLATE 23. A Victorian style
of the Romantic period "in
the modern manner." The
color scheme employed to
delight the modern eye
would have been appalling
to the taste of the nineteenth
century. Arranged by Mrs.
Jack C. Fuson.

PLATE 25. An old-fashioned,
sentimental look takes off in
a new direction in this
massed-line arrangement.

PLATE 26. A clear definition of contrast in the use of vertical and horizontal lines appears in the modern style. The vertical column of the modern stonêware container is continued with the tall stem of butterfly weed. Weathered wood accentuates the horizontal jutting lines of the container, repeated again by the old chestnut board base. The lily brings it all into focus. Designer, Mrs. Benjamin S. Killmaster.

PLATE 27. Sagebrush and and roses in free style. Designer, Mrs. Myles H. Reynolds.

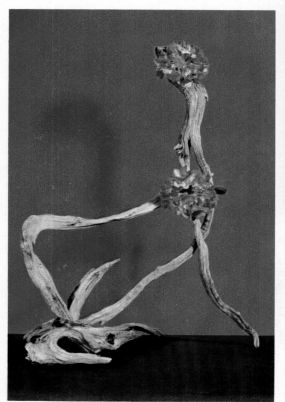

PLATE 28. Heavy lines in a striking outline enclose a volume of space in this abstract design. Circular patterns of rhododendron blossoms are interestingly placed as contrasting design elements. Designer, Mrs. Myles H. Reynolds.

If stems are wired before flowers are dried, the handling of many kinds through the drying, storing and arranging procedures is greatly facilitated. The hazards of breaking, drooping and collapsing are eliminated. Wiring can best be accomplished when flowers are fresh. It is generally impossible to insert wire into stems or flower heads after they are dry for they are all but impenetrable—except, of course, for hollow stems.

SUBSTITUTE STEMS

Ideally, all flowers would appear in arrangements on their own stems; however, to be able to dry large flowers easily in a face-up position, the stems must be cut off and wires, which can be bent up out of the way, substituted. If a desirable length of stem were kept, the necessary depth of the covering medium would be impractical, or a complicated procedure would be required.

REINFORCED STEMS

Stems of flowers that collapse while drying in a face-down position, such as zinnias and black-eyed Susans, can be supported by inserting wire through the stem into the calyx or head. Thus, the natural stem becomes sturdy and straight and does not fall over where it emerges from the covering medium.

Flower stems that are fragile after they are dried, such as hyacinth, can be reinforced with wire even though they are dried in a horizontal position.

Wire can be inserted to lengthen a stem that, in all probability, could not be done without breaking the flower after it is dried.

WIRE

Annealed, green-painted florist wire is a recommended type as it is easy and pleasant to handle and does not rust. The 24-gauge wire is practical for most purposes since it is strong enough to support all but the very heavy flowers, and light enough for all but the most delicate. When selecting wire it may be helpful to know that the lower gauge numbers identify the heavier weights, and the higher numbers the lighter weights.

WIRE CUTTERS

Lightweight wire cutters of the chain nose mechanic's pliers type are an almost indispensable tool. The cutting edge, located in about the center of the head of the instrument is only one of its serviceable features. The tip of the serrated nose proves quite useful as forceps for the delicate operation of placing flowers in arrangements where space is limited or when working with miniature arrangements.

LENGTH OF WIRE

Wires are usually cut in six-inch lengths which facilitates the handling of flowers through the various processes of covering, uncovering, storing and arranging. A longer wire is awkward and will become bent. A shorter length will be necessary if flowers are dried in a covered tin when using the silica gel method of drying according to directions of the manufacturer.

Figure 49.
Wiring
short stems.

FACE-UP POSITION *Techniques*
for Wiring

Large flowers, such as full-blown roses or tulips, necessitate cutting stems short. Enough stem length is needed to allow for a firm grip to hold the flower while inserting the wire up through the stem into the calyx or flower head. The stem shrinks as it dries holding the wire securely in place. There is no need to insert the wire deeply into the blossom, which might mutilate it.

FACE-DOWN POSITION

Flowers can be dried with longer stems. Three to five inches is adequate for most arrangements. The hook method should be used for flowers with hollow stems, such as zinnias. For flowers, such as black-eyed Susan and daisies, the wire needs only to be inserted just into the head. The wire will protrude if pushed into the flower too far, because of shrinkage during the drying process. It may be necessary to straighten the stem to insert a wire into the base of the flower. After this is done bend the wired stem to recover the original curve.

Figure 50. Reinforcing long stems.

Hook Technique

For flowers, such as dahlias and those with hollow stems, such as zinnias, it is advisable to use a hook to hold the wire securely. Insert the wire through the stem up through the center of the flower until it protrudes an inch or so. Bend it to form a small hook. Pull the wire back down until the hook is firmly embedded in the bloom.

Figure 51.

Insertion Technique

When wire is inserted through long stems that are not hollow, the task is sometimes difficult. Begin the insertion in the center and try to keep it there. If it sticks out the side, pull back and try to guide the stem into the path of the wire. Should the wire become bent, pull it out and start again with the other end or with a new wire. It may be necessary to shorten the stem. When a wire cannot be coaxed up through a stem, begin by inserting the wire into the center of the bloom from the top, make a hook and pull it into place.

Wiring may seem a tedious extra chore, but untold advantages can be recognized. Flowers appearing in arrangements on their own natural stems in which the wire is concealed add to the quality and beauty. If wire must be attached after stems are dried in order to support them, it is unattractive.

If head of flowers droop after they are placed in arrangements because the stem is weak and cannot support the flower, its beauty is lost. Wired stems can be bent so that flowers can be made to assume any desired pose. Graceful curves are easily obtained. Substitute wires can be slipped into natural stems or covered with tape.

Gluing

Most flowers that are dried in sand or silica gel can be uncovered intact. If a petal is lost, it can easily be replaced with a touch of glue. However, a few flowers are inclined to lose some petals or shatter completely. This danger is increased for those prone to this habit when they are sand-dried for sand is the heavier medium. If one is determined to dry these kinds successfully, they can be glued before covering.

Single flowers, such as roses and dahlias and some daisies, will often drop some petals during the uncovering procedure, or when they are handled after they are dry. This occurs regardless of the method used.

All roses, except for those in tight bud, will fall apart when they are uncovered after having been dried in sand, making it necessary to glue them before they are covered when using the sand-drying method. Any white all-purpose glue that dries fast and is transparent when dry is adequate.

To replace a lost petal, dip its base in the glue and replace it in its original position. Hold the flower or support it in some manner so that the force of gravity will help to hold it in position until the glue dries. Just the smallest touch of glue is all that is needed.

When flowers are glued before drying, the glue must be allowed to dry thoroughly, which requires a half hour or longer. To keep flowers fresh and turgid, put the stems back into water after the glue has been applied.

Glue will flow better if it is diluted with about an equal amount of water. Squeeze a few drops onto a sheet of wax paper, add the water and mix. The small tip of a camel's hair water color brush is an excellent tool for this purpose. Apply a *thin* coat at the base of the petal with a short stroke to spread it evenly.

For single flowers, an application at the back between the petals and the sepals at the calyx will be sufficient.

For double roses, particularly those that are more than three-quarters open, several rows of petals must be glued. The application should be made only where it is possible to reach the petal's base. Generally not all rows must be glued.

Figure 52.

To prevent smearing the surface, some petals can be pulled back carefully so that the tip of the brush can be inserted to reach the base. This can probably be done best by holding the stem between the thumb and the middle finger so the index finger is free. Care must be taken that manipulation of the petals does not spoil the shape. For careful application, it may be helpful to rest one's arms against a table or the arm of a chair to steady the hand.

NOTE: The amount of glue seen in the photographs is greatly in excess of that required. The amount shown was only for the purpose of making it visible in the area where it should be applied.

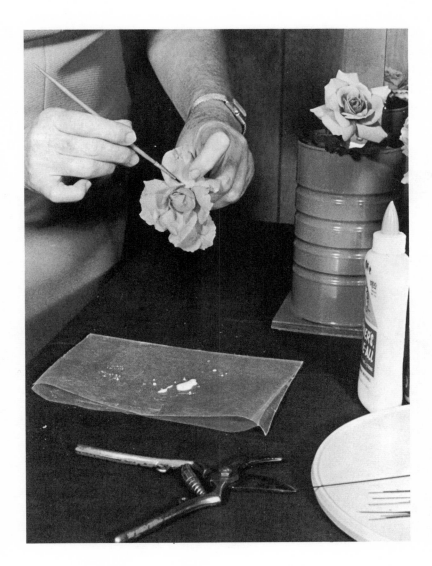

Figure 53.

Covering
Techniques

FACE-UP POSITION

To retain the characteristic form of flowers, such as roses, peonies, marigolds, dahlias and tulips, it is necessary to cover each flower in a face-up position. The petal arrangement of flowers, as well as the natural shape of each petal and special features, such as prominent stamens and open disk flowers, can be preserved best in this position. In this way it is possible for one to observe and control the flow of the covering medium (sand or silica gel) in order to support all parts of the flower with equal pressure until it is dehydrated, becomes crisp and will hold its shape.

Large double flowers. Pour a base of the medium in which the flowers are to be dried in one end of the box or tin where the flowers are to be placed. The depth of the base is determined by the size of the flower and the length of the stem. It should be deep enough, however, to support the lower petals and hold the flower in an upright position. Cut the stem the desired length, insert a wire, and bend it

Figure 54.

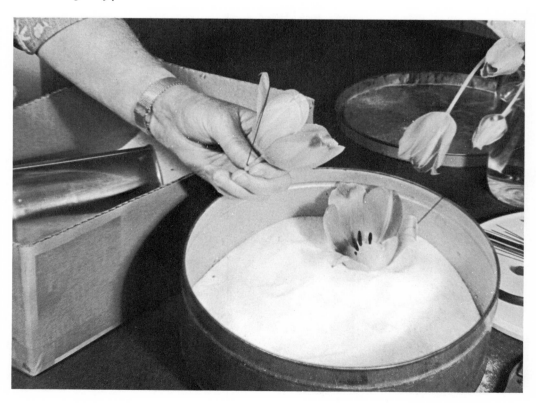

Figure 55.

up at a right angle. Anchor the flowers in the medium spacing each flower at least one inch from other flowers and the sides of the container. Sometimes this can best be done by pulling back the sand with the fingers of one hand to make a depression while positioning the flower. Begin covering the flowers by pouring the medium to fill the spaces between the flowers and/or the container. Pour carefully to build up around each flower so that it flows under and over the outer petals. (If each flower or row is completely covered before the next is added, the depth of the medium interferes with placing others.) Then place additional flowers until the container is filled. Continue to cover by building up to surround each petal, row by row. The medium flows into the center thus supporting all in their natural position as the depth increases. One should not begin to pour, sprinkle or sift directly on the flower, but rather build up the medium to cover with equal pressure by pouring from side to side. With practice one can develop skill in adjusting the flow so that the pressure will be evenly distributed and the flowers can be covered without disturbing the position of a single petal.

However, should too much pressure distort a petal's shape while covering, the medium may be pulled away with one's fingers releasing enough pressure to let the petals assume their natural position again before continuing. If petal edges curl decidedly, it may be necessary to lift each one slightly so that the medium can flow under to preserve the curve, rather than having the edge pressed flat. The handle of a camel's hair brush is an excellent tool for this purpose.

Single flowers. For flowers with deep cups, such as tulips and single peonies, the medium must be built up evenly by pouring back and forth between the outside and the center to keep the pressure on the petals equalized.

Figure 56.
Diagonal position,
face up.

DIAGONAL POSITION

This position with flowers facing upward but not necessarily perpendicular can be used for smaller flowers and buds. This makes it possible to retain a longer natural stem without increasing the depth of the covering medium to the extent that it is unmanageable. A ridge is built with the medium, then a row of flower stems is anchored (wired or not as required) along the ridge with the head hanging free. Cover-

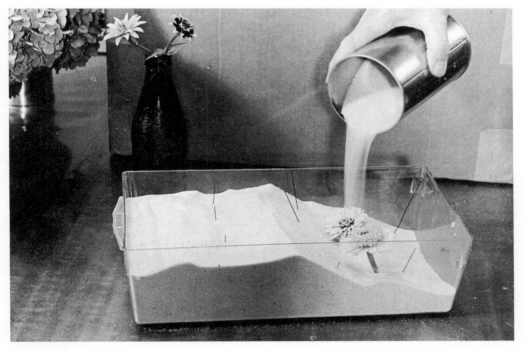

Figure 57.

ing is begun by pouring between the flowers to fill the spaces along the ridge at the back of the flowers; then from side to side and in front to distribute the pressure evenly as for the other face-up positions; then proceeding with the second row as before. Love-in-a-mist, marigolds, geum, Mexicana or Persian jewel zinnias, cornflowers, small roses and windflowers, and still other flowers, can be placed to dry in this position to preserve a longer natural stem.

FACE-DOWN POSITION

Single daisy-type flowers and flowers with their inflorescence on a plane, such as Queen Anne's lace, can best be covered to support the petals by placing them in a face-down position.

It is important to note the shape of the flower faces and support them accordingly so that the characteristic form can be retained. Pour the medium to cover the bottom of the container and prepare the base to fit the face of the flower; flat faces should rest on flat bases, concave faces on a mound, and convex faces would require a depression into which they could be fitted. When black-eyed Susans or rudbeckia are placed face-down, a depression can be made with the finger tip in the base in which to fit the cone.

Each stem is cut 3 to 5 inches in length and a wire is inserted up through the stem into the calyx or base of the flower. Remember not to push the wire too far or it will show when the flower dries. If

Figure 58.

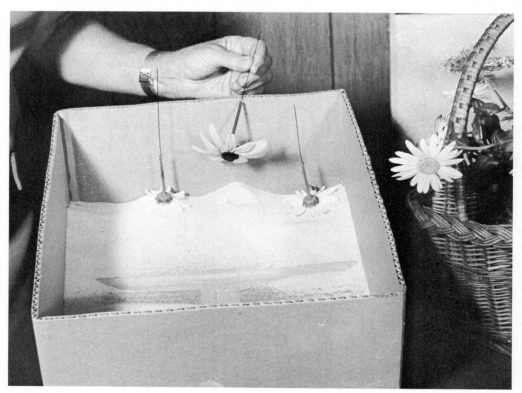

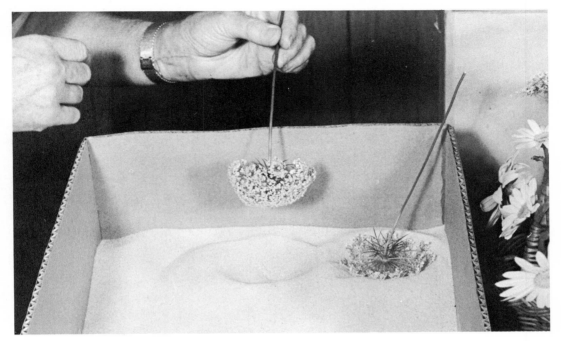

Figure 59.

necessary, the flower may be steadied on its prepared base by holding the wire with one hand while pouring enough of the medium to build up around and cover to hold it in position. When two or three rows are in place, the first rows are completely and evenly covered. If each flower is completely covered when placed, the depth of the medium interferes with the placement of additional flowers. When the container is filled the covering medium should be poured to a uniform depth, but only enough to cover completely so that it will not shift when moved. When covering a flower with more than one row of petals, such as zinnias, the medium should be poured around it and built up to flow between the petals as in the face-up method. This will preserve the natural curve of the petals and maintain the third dimensional qualities of the flower.

Spray type, such as feverfew. Stems are sturdy and do not need to be wired. Select a small lateral or terminal spray and hold head down so that the flower or flowers at the top rest on a light base of the medium. Cover these flowers with enough medium to hold the spray in position, then place another spray until the container is filled. Continue to cover by building up the medium so that the flowers at different levels on the stems of the sprays are completely covered.

Cluster type, such as butterfly weed and hydrangea. The bottom of a deep box is covered to a depth of about one-half inch. The stems are sturdy and do not need to be wired. One should remove the leaves from the lower part of the stem and arrange the sprays in the container leaning the stems against the sides to stabilize them. While lifting one spray at a time by the stem slightly above the base, the medium is poured to fill the spaces, building up the level to flow under, into and over each floret until the spray is supported in position. Once all the sprays are supported they can then be evenly and completely covered. Clusters of hydrangea may be separated and covered face-down by pouring sand in the spaces between the clusters and through them to completely cover.

Figure 60.

HORIZONTAL POSITION

Elongated forms, such as larkspur, delphinium, snapdragons and lilac, can be covered in a horizontal position. The stems of these flowers require no additional support.

A layer of covering medium is poured to cover the bottom of the box or tin. Flowers are arranged in the container leaving space enough to pour the medium around and between them until it builds up to flow under, around, between and into each individual flower to support them as in the face-up method. The flower can be lifted slightly as the flow of sand is started to flow under so that the bottom petals are not mashed from the pressure of lying flat. Pour first on one side, then on the other, to equalize the pressure of the medium as it is built up to cover the flowers. It is often advisable to lift the tips of the petals which have a decided curve when covering so the medium can flow under. This prevents their being bent or creased. The small plastic handle of a camel's hair brush is a good tool for this operation.

Figure 61.

Flowering branches, such as dogwood, can be placed with the flowers face-up. Fill spaces first, building up to cover the individual flowers.

SPECIAL POSITIONS

For flowers such as lilies, each flower can be held with one hand while pouring the medium to cover and support it. By pouring to distribute the pressure evenly, all parts can be covered without changing the natural shape.

LABELING

A label bearing the date and kind of flowers for each flower-filled container is required for identification and timing.

SOUFFLÉ COLLAR

When flowers are preserved by the "quick-drying method," the depth of the container can be increased for large flowers, such as magnolias, with the use of a soufflé collar. A piece of lightweight cardboard can be cut to line the side of the tin and extend above it. Two pieces may be taped together for the required length. If the regular silica gel method is used, a deeper container will be needed so that a lid can be used during the drying process.

Uncovering Techniques

Removal of flowers and foliage from the covering medium requires care to prevent breakage. Perhaps patience is also required when waiting for flowers to dry when using the sand-drying method.

The box in which the flowers are buried is tipped to allow the sand to flow slowly from one corner into a storage box. As the flow continues, flowers will be released and each one can be caught and lifted out as it becomes free. Pulling generally causes petals to be broken off. The direction of removal should follow that of the movement of the sand. Perhaps it may seem that one person does not possess enough hands for this operation. For a beginner, it might be wise to enlist the help of some willing accomplice. Small flowers, such as feverfew, can be pulled out gently by the stem.

Flowers dried in silica gel can be uncovered in the same manner by letting the silica gel flow into a box or tin used only for this purpose. When removed, flowers can be placed carefully in one end of the box used for "sandblasting." The residue should then be removed. (See "Grooming and Cosmetics.")

Figure 62. Note that open boxes allow evaporation of moisture in the sand-drying method.

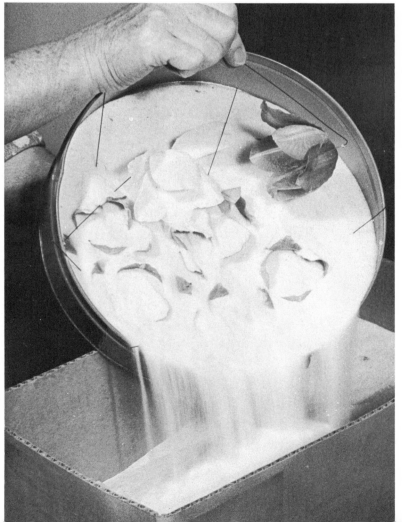

Figure 63. Sealable tins are used for silica gel method.

Dried flowers are fragile and must be protected from breakage, disfiguration and excessive moisture in the air when removed from the drying medium. If thoroughly dry, they should be stored immediately. (See "Storing.") If not completely dry, flowers should be placed so that there is no pressure to distort the form. If round or daisy forms lie on their sides they will become bent. Wired or natural stems can be stuck into a block of floral foam temporarily. Where conditions of low humidity do not exist, lay the flowers on top of the silica gel in a container as there is no need to cover the flower again, just close and seal the container and set aside for a day or two.

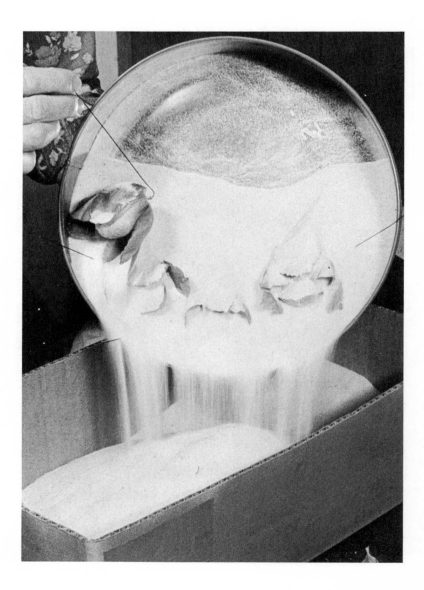

Figure 64.

6   Grooming and Cosmetics

Flowers must show no trace of any material used to preserve them and appear at their best. When removed from sand, they are clean and lovely except for those with a pronounced velvety texture, such as some delphinium, and those with hairy surfaces, such as stems and tips of snapdragon. Silica gel, unfortunately, leaves a residue which should be removed so that flowers will look their best. Even more important, clinging particles will absorb moisture from the air and affect the flower's stability. Residue can be removed with a camel's hair artist's brush or by a new and extraordinarily effective method "sandblasting."

"SANDBLASTING"

To remove the residue, hold the flower over a large box containing a medium quantity of sand. From this box scoop a handful and allow a light stream to fall from a height of twelve to fifteen inches to strike the flower petals. Turn the flower so that all surfaces are reached and to keep weight from building up which might break off petals. As the grains strike, roll and bounce off, any residue is carried with them. All traces can be removed from intricately structured flowers by this method since the falling grains can reach all surfaces. The large box is suggested because bouncing grains of sand scatter widely.

(WARNING)—Sand used for removing silica gel must be kept separate from that used to dry flowers. Place a conspicuous reminder in the box of sand for this purpose. If silica gel becomes mixed with sand, this mixture must then be handled as silica gel alone. Remember it absorbs moisture from the air and must be kept sealed and be dried out before using it to dry flowers.

The "sandblasting" method is used effectively to remove residue, if any, from flowers that have been sand-dried. The regular storage box can be used.

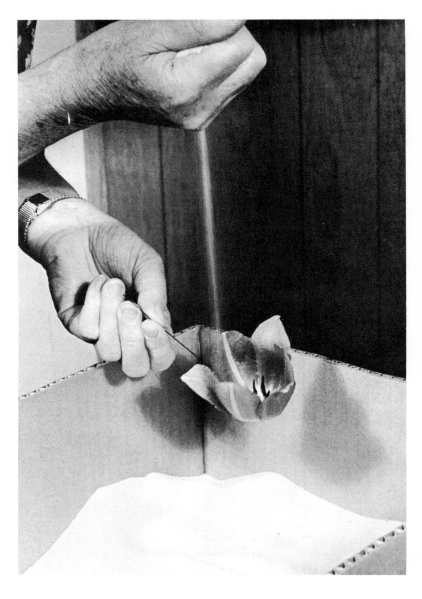

Figure 65.

Figure 66.

Manual Method for Cleaning

It is disconcerting to find that sand will cling to the surface where glue is applied before flowers are dried, even when glue is thoroughly dry, as should be the case before flowers are covered. This can be removed by rubbing with the side of a slender camel's hair brush handle, or with the smooth tip of the handle. The camel's hair brush itself may also be used as required for cleaning residue from the petal surface.

STEAMING

Restores fresh appearance to air-dried material. *Celosia plumosa* will assume its natural feathery, graceful form by this means. While holding the plume in the billowy steam it may be necessary to tap the stem against the side of the kettle to loosen the plume. When held at an angle after steaming any desired curve is formed as the tip quickly dries. Strawflowers, statice and other air-dried flowers that may have been crushed will be rejuvenated by steaming.

RECONDITIONING MATERIAL

Some dried and preserved material that has been used in an arrangement can be satisfactorily revived. Some of this material, especially celosia, may have changed color from exposure to light and have an even more beautiful tone than it originally possessed. Steam will fluff plumes, restore curves, straighten stems, clean and revive many kinds of air-dried material. Some kinds, such as sea oats, pods, berries and strawflowers can also be quickly washed by swishing in suds and rinsing in clear water. Gently shake off water and pat dry. Flowers dried in sand or silica gel cannot be subjected to these treatments. Foliage preserved with glycerine can also be washed, rinsed and polished with a cloth to remove dust.

Cosmetic Use of Spray Paints

Spray paints with a matte or dull finish developed for use on fresh flowers can sometimes be used for dried flowers and foliage to good advantage. Green spray paint will restore a fresh appearance. Chlorophyll, which gives the green color to leaves and ferns, disintegrates when exposed to light, either direct sunlight or artificial light. This is more rapid in ferns and leaves of delicate substance, such as maidenhair fern or leaves of columbine. Choice of shade is generally most pleasing when it approximates the natural color—moss-green or olive-green. Some of the spray paint colors are too intense and give an artificial look. Some leaves preserved in glycerine can be lightly sprayed with green to give them back their original color. In reconditioning, spray paint can be used to give new life to some kinds of material; jonquil-yellow makes goldenrod bright again, and a burst of red on rough-textured celosia may make a magenta hue more pleasing.

Clear spray paints used by artists to protect charcoal drawings, pastels and tempera are sometimes suggested to protect flowers from dampness or to prevent shattering. This has not proven effective in a humid climate. It is perhaps better to protect flowers by careful storing and use them in arrangements only in heated or air-conditioned rooms. Shattering is minimized by drying before flowers reach maturity.

Painted material for special color effects is accepted and used in contemporary design.

Precautions should be exercised when using spray paints for they are flammable and also leave a powdery residue. Use according to directions on the can.

Storing

Storing of air-dried material is no problem since it can be left hanging where it was dried or placed in boxes or plastic bags in any convenient dry place.

Storing is the part of the whole process of preserving flowers in sand or silica gel that is the most tedious; however, it is a most important part. The flowers are amazingly beautiful in form and color when they are first removed from the drying medium. Careful storing will be required to keep them in this state until they are placed in the flower arrangement.

Flowers must be protected from excessive humidity to keep them crisp and dry and to prevent them from absorbing moisture and becoming limp and wilted. They must also be protected from bright light, to keep the colors from fading, and from dust, to keep them clean. Care should also be taken to prevent flowers from becoming broken or deformed during the period when they are stored.

In damp climates a workroom equipped with a dehumidifier provides an ideal storage area. A setting of 60 per cent will protect all but the most extremely perishable flowers.

Airtight containers can provide protective storage if a suitable storage area is not available. They also protect flowers from dust and damage. Tin cans and plastic boxes should be sealed with tape. Cardboard boxes can be placed in plastic bags and fastened securely. Additional protection for extremely perishable flowers can be provided by placing a small paper cup half filled with silica gel to absorb any moisture in the container holding the flowers.

Place flowers in containers for storing to prevent breakage and disfigurement. Flowers that have been dried in a face-up position, such as roses, marigolds and small zinnias, can be stored in the same position. The wire should not be straightened, but should remain bent at a right angle. This helps to keep the flower from resting on its side and becoming bent.

Figure 67.

Flowers that have been dried in a face-down position, such as daisies, large zinnias and rudbeckia, must have the wired stem supported so that the petals do not rest on the bottom of the box and become disfigured. The support can be fashioned of paper rolled into a tube about one inch in diameter and long enough to fit securely across the width of the box. Prop the wire on the tube so that the bloom does not touch the bottom or sides of the box. Fill the whole row in this manner, then place another tube over the ends of the wires and fill the next row. All of the flowers should be securely held in place when stored in this manner. They may also be stored in an upright position by placing stems in floral foam.

Figure 68.

Face-down position for storing lilies and large tulips will keep the anthers of the lilies and tulips from collapsing and the petals of tulips from spreading open. Blocks of floral foam, about two inches thick, can be taped into a deep cardboard box. The wired stems inserted into the foam support the blooms to best advantage.

Flowers dried in a horizontal position pose no problem since they can be stored in that same position.

The arrangements themselves can be stored in boxes if the container is anchored so that it will not shift. The box must be wrapped in a plastic bag and sealed so that it is airtight. Silica gel can be added for extra protection.

Transporting
Arrangements   To take dried arrangements, as gifts or exhibits, by automobile, airplane or train, it is necessary to prevent damage to them en route. Because dried flowers are fragile, certainly not pliable, and even perishable, definite precautions are necessary.

Adequate space is required so that the tallest airy tip will not come in contact with any surface. The container must be stabilized by some means to keep the arrangement from falling or sliding, thereby crushing the flowers.

Figure 69.

If carried in the trunk or on the floor of the automobile, sand bags can be used to hold the container in place. Shallow cardboard boxes to which the container is securely bound by strapping tape will serve to stabilize the arrangement. If the length and width of the box is greater than that of the three-dimensional arrangement, marginal space for it on each side insures protection; and, if the weather is damp, they can sit "as passengers" on the back seat in a heated or air-conditioned car. In

Figure 70.

a station wagon, heavy objects, such as bricks, placed on the outside will keep the box from sliding around. Drive carefully!

Better protection is afforded if the arrangement is enclosed in a cardboard carton. To be able to put an arrangement into a box without breaking the flowers, one side of the carton can be cut open, and with the panel laid out flat the arrangement can easily be slipped in from the side. Fasten the container securely to the bottom with Davee tape or strapping tape, so it will not slip or fall over, as shown in Figure 70. Fasten the side panel back into position. Boxed arrangements may be carried in the car or taken by air.

To protect the arrangement from dampness, it must be boxed as described, then covered with a plastic bag and sealed, or tied with colorful yarn gift tie with a bow at the top. The addition of a small quantity of silica gel to absorb moisture is an added protection. This is also a good way to store a dried arrangement.

Part Three

A CONCISE GUIDE TO
BEST METHODS AND HINTS
FOR 155 VARIETIES

Good candidates for flower preservation appear in the arrangements illustrated in this book. These, along with some others with which the author has had experience, are included in the Flower Guide.

Recommended method or methods for each kind of plant material, positions for covering, and the advisability of wiring or gluing certain kinds before drying are listed. A brief description, the best stage of development, and an observation concerning flowers that are not stable under conditions of humidity above 60 per cent are also included.

Drying time for the sand-drying method has not been given for there is no need for urgent removal. About ten days to two weeks is required, depending on drying conditions and kinds of flowers.

Timing is mandatory when the silica gel method is used. The exact time required depends on a number of factors (see Part Two), but the approximate time given should serve quite well until experience suggests refinements.

It is advisable to experiment with many kinds and varieties of plant material. Since the characteristics of flowers differ so widely in substance, texture, color and structure, some varieties can be successfully dried while others are dismal failures. It is hoped that many kinds that the author has found difficult or not had the opportunity to try will be successfully preserved by others.

ACACIA. Air-dry.
> A tropical shrub bearing very small yellow flowers in dense finger-shaped or globular clusters. Dries deep gold or mustard color. Blooms March or April—available at florist shops.

ACHILLEA (Yarrow).
> A. *ptarmica* (The Pearl). Sand; horizontal.
> This is a double-flowered variety with small flower heads that remain white. Dry small spray of flower clusters.

ACROCLINIUM (*Helipterum roseum*) (see Everlastings). Air-dry.
> Resembles strawflowers but daintier in form and of more pastel colors— salmon, apricot, pink, rose, red, white and creamy tones. Pick while in bud. Can be used with natural stems, but wiring before drying prevents drooping of heads when used in arrangements.

ADIANTUM (see Maidenhair Fern).

AGERATUM *houstonianum* (Floss Flower). Sand or silica gel; face-up or face-down.

   Annual hybrid blooms are fluffy, compact flower clusters of powdery-blue ranging to deep blue; also white and pink. Most blues dry on the lavender side. Silica gel: 2–3 days; "quick-dry": 12–18 hours.

   Hardy or perennial Ageratum (Mist Flower). This is not *Ageratum* as the common names implies but *Eupatorium coelestinum*. It is similar, but taller, and blooms later. Air-day, sand or silica gel. Silica gel: 3–4 days; "quick-dry": 12–18 hours.

ALLIUM (Ornamental Onion). Air-dry, sand or silica gel; head-down; wire.

   Small flowers are usually clustered in round heads of varying sizes and colors. The blossom can be dried in silica gel: 4–5 days; "quick-dry": 18–24 hours. The seed heads, also attractive, can be left to mature on the plant and should be collected before the seeds pop. A few attractive varieties are:

   A. *aflatunense*—dense spherical heads of lilac-purple.

   A. *albopilosum* (syn. *Christophii*)—large umbels up to 10 inches with star-shaped violet flowers.

   A. *azureum*—tall growing with small compact heads, blue blossom.

   A. *giganteum*—large round heads of violet flowers.

   A. *Schoenoprasum* (chives)—small lavender blossom.

   A. *Schubertii*—handsome seed head with long radiating pedicels is very attractive.

ALTHAEA   (see Hollyhock).

AMMOBIUM *alatum grandiflorum* (Winged Everlasting). Air-dry.

   Small heads of silvery-white bracts. Pick while in bud.

ANCHUSA   (see Forget-me-not).

ANEMONE *coronaria* (Poppy Anemone). Silica gel or sand; face-up; wire.

   The modern hybrids of the De Caen and St. Brigid varieties are easily grown in the garden. Large, brilliantly colored flowers are available in the florist shops from January through March.

   Cut the stem just below the fringe of finely cut leaves and insert a wire just into the flower. Silica gel: 3–4 days; or dry by "quick-dry" method for best results: 12–18 hours; or when sand is used will dry with good color at room temperature in a week to ten days. Colors are wonderfully retained except for dulling of red, and any blue in rose is accentuated. Protect from humidity in excess of 60 per cent.

   A. *japonica* (Windflower).   Silica gel or sand; face-up.

   These fall-blooming, perennials are lovely in the garden. Cut to dry when first open for best substance. Lovely, dainty flowers for mass arrangements. Protect from above-average humidity, especially during storage. Silica gel: 2–3 days; "quick-dry": 8–12 hours.

ANTHEMIS (Chamomile)   (see Daisy). Sand; face-down; wire.

   Daisy-like flowers with heads 1 to 2 inches, gold or pale yellow. Generally, dry excessively in silica gel.

AQUILEGIA   (see Columbine).

ARTEMISIA. Air-dry or sand.

Interesting gray foliage material. Sand-drying, of course, will preserve the beauty and grace of the deeply cut foliage in best form.

ARTICHOKE (*Cynara Scolymus*). Silica gel; "quick-dry"; face-up; wire.

This vegetable, known as globe artichoke, takes on the appearance of an exotic flower of bold form when the scales are pressed open to dry and assume the petal arrangement of a full-blown rose. If the artichoke is allowed to stand in the open air until it becomes somewhat wilted, the scales can be more easily manipulated. Insert a wire into the stem and anchor face-up in silica gel in a container of adequate size to accommodate it when fully opened (a soufflé collar may be used). Beginning with the outside row, force the scales apart row by row by pressing silica gel between them with the fingers. When the desired shape is obtained, cover completely with silica gel. "Quick-dry," 24–30 hours. If the regular silica gel method is used, it will be necessary to pour off the silica gel in four or five days and replace it with dry because the scales are so fleshy one application is not sufficient to effect dehydration.

ASTER (Fall Aster) (see Michaelmas Daisy).

To many gardeners this name implies the garden or China aster, which does not belong to the genus *Aster* but to the genus *Callistephus*. China asters shatter excessively so cannot be considered among the better kinds for preserving.

ASTILBE. Air-dry by hanging, sand or silica gel; horizontal.

Hybrids are fine plants having delicate spire-like clusters of white, pink and garnet colors which dry to beige and muted colors. Silica gel: 3–4 days.

AZALEA. Silica gel; face-up.

These flowers can be dried with good form, but the delicate petals often appear translucent and collapse under average room conditions. Deciduous kinds are more stable, but must still be protected from dampness. Silica gel: 3–4 days; "quick-dry": 12–18 hours.

BABY'S BREATH (*Gypsophila*). Air-dry.

G. *paniculata* is the best-known perennial species. Its delicate, airy qualities make it useful for contemporary as well as period arrangements. The new larger double-flowered and some pink varieties can be sand-dried so as to preserve the perfect form of the individual flower for use in miniature bouquets. Pick when in full bloom and hang in warm, dry place to dry quickly; to preserve white and prevent cream coloring, store in dry, dark place.

BACHELOR'S BUTTON (*Centaurea Cyanus*). Silica gel; face-up.

Should be picked the first day the flower is open to insure that the petals will not drop. This small flower comes in many colors and is most useful in many styles of arrangements. Silica gel method is best for good color and to prevent shattering: 2–3 days; "quick-dry": 8–12 hours.

BAPTISIA *australis* (Blue False Indigo). Foliage—Glycerine.

About August foliage is mature and can be preserved by the glycerine method, resulting in a steel-gray color. Becomes limp if too saturated. Seed pods are handsome and also steel-gray in color. Pick these about August when they have their best color.

BARBERRY (*Berberis*). Glycerine.

B. julianae is a favorite of many flower arrangers. Cut those branches that have a beauty of line and characteristic whorls of leaves. Their spines can be removed before treating to make handling more pleasant.

BEECH (*Fagus grandifolia*) (American Beech). Glycerine and press.

F. sylvatica (European Beech). Beech branches have interesting, graceful lines with the leaves of good size and shape for arrangements of many styles. Glycerine-preserved green leaves of American beech turn dark green then dark brown in time, while leaves just beginning to turn yellow in the fall will become russet-brown. Pressed leaves will retain their autumn color well but should be pressed as they begin to change color to prevent them from falling from the branch after they have dried.

The leaves of the various beeches dried by pressing retain their variety of colors.

The seed pods of the beech are also attractive and should not be overlooked.

BERRIES.

The fruits of many plants are attractive. Those that are hard to the touch, such as Nandina berries, and those of the Blackberry Lily, retain their beauty and are the most useful for arrangements. Soft berries are perishable. Pick when mature but not overripe.

BLACKBERRY LILY (*Belamcanda chinensis*). Air-dry.

Seed pods, which resemble a blackberry, are attractive and different. Cut them when the seed pods start to split open and the shiny black seeds can first be seen.

BLACK-EYED SUSAN (*Rudbeckia hirta*) (see Daisy). Sand; face-down; wire.

These flowers grow wild in the fields and can be easily dried and used with good effect in many arrangements. They retain their bright golden color and charming daisy-like form for a long time. When picking, select those with the broader ray petals for more pleasing appearance when dried. When placing face-down in sand, make an indentation in the sand into which the center cone will fit allowing the ray petals to lie flat on the layer of sand before starting to cover. (See "Storing.")

BLUEBERRY (*Vaccinium corymbosum* in the North, and *V. virgatum* in the South). Foliage—Press or glycerine.

The foliage of these varieties have small, attractive leaves that can be pressed to keep their green color and also their autumn color of rusty-red. If preserved in glycerine, the leaves turn dark green and then brown after a period of time if cut when green. If preserved when the leaves start to assume their autumn color, they turn russet-brown.

BONESET or THOROUGHWORT (*Eupatorium perfoliatum*). Air-dry.

These dense flat-topped clusters of small white flower heads often grow in the fields where goldenrod grows. Pick and hang to dry in August when partially open. Clusters can be separated for use as filler material in mass arrangements.

BOUGAINVILLEA. Silica gel; horizontal.

A complete cluster can be covered. Silica gel: 3–4 days; "quick-dry": 12–18 hours.

BUTTERCUP (*Ranunculus repens pleniflorus*, also called *R. speciosus*). Sand or silica gel; face-up or diagonal to retain the natural stem.

This variety is a double-flowered creeping form with flowers about three-fourths of an inch wide. It is a dainty flower that keeps its gold color well and is most useful in many arrangements. The single wild buttercup can be dried but is not as stable as the variety mentioned here. Silica gel: 2–3 days; "quick-dry": 8–12 hours.

BUTTERFLY-WEED (*Asclepias tuberosa*). Sand or silica gel; face-down or horizontal.

This showiest of all native milkweeds grows wild in the fields and along the roadside. It can also be grown in the garden and is listed in seed catalogues. For interesting contrast of form and color, cut to dry when the tips of the clusters are still in bud. The clusters of orange flowers are interestingly branched and can be dried face-down in a large box, with the added advantage of retaining the natural long stems which are rigid enough to stand upright during the drying process. When dried in a horizontal position more leaves can be dried to keep their natural shape. Both the flowers and leaves have a more exciting color when dried in silica gel—"quick-dry": 8–12 hours; silica gel: 2–3 days. Color changes occur after exposure to light. Careful spraying with orange will cover the purple color that the flower acquires. (See "Cosmetic Use of Spray Paints" and "Grooming and Cosmetics.")

CAMELLIA. Sand or silica gel; face-up.

C. japonica. Excellent form when dried but true color is not retained; however, markings occur that make it interesting and exotic.

C. sasanqua. Flower is more stable if dried when first open. Some varieties are more successful than others. Silica gel 4–5 days; "quick-dry": 18–24 hours.

CANTERBURY BELLS (*Campanula Medium*). Silica gel; horizontal.

Charming and unusual form with good color. Silica gel: 3–4 days; "quick-dry": 12–18 hours.

CARNATIONS (*Dianthus Caryophyllus*). Sand or silica gel; face-up.

"Florist carnations" can be satisfactorily preserved, both the large flowered and the miniature. These can also be grown in the garden. Colors are variable. Silica gel: 3 days; "quick-dry": 12–18 hours.

CAT-TAIL (*Typha latifolia*). Pick at desired stage before fully mature.

After drying at brown stage they should be dipped in alcohol and shellac (half and half) or sprayed with glue to prevent shattering.

CELOSIA *cristata* (Cockscomb). Air-dry.

Pick to dry as seeds start to ripen.

The interesting, often fantastic or grotesque forms can be used quite effectively in contemporary arrangements. Many new varieties of cockscomb contribute to a growing range of color, from brilliant orange-red to light chartreuse. The colors change when the flowers are dried but exciting and useful variations in hues result. The smaller flower clusters are very useful in mass arrangements, contributing a different form and texture. The larger clusters can be broken apart for this use. These flowers remain beautiful for long periods of time.

C. *plumosa* (Prince's Feather). Air-dry.

The silky plumes of this plant possess the durable quality and varied color range of the cockscombs. When dried the plumes become matted. Their delightful natural form, however, is not lost since steaming will restore their feathery appearance. (See "Grooming and Cosmetics.")

Celosia not only changes color during the drying process, but subtle color changes occur over a period of time upon exposure to light. These changes are generally delightful. When arrangements are dismantled after use, these flowers can be saved, steamed again to clean and fluff, and placed to great advantage in a new arrangement. Some red shades can be exposed to light after they are dried to acquire a more pleasing color and used with more pleasure a year later.

Stems of Celosia *plumosa*—air-dry. Very valuable as substitute stems. The soft interior of the stems will hold delicate short stems securely when they are inserted.

CHRISTMAS ROSE and LENTEN ROSE   (see *Helleborus*).

CHRYSANTHEMUM. Silica gel; face-up.

Many varieties are available, but not many make satisfactory dried flowers as most shatter. Perhaps varieties not available to the author would be more successful. (Feverfew, Shasta Daisies and Marguerites are successful and are listed separately.) Silica gel: 3–4 days; "quick-dry": 12–18 hours.

CLEMATIS. Sand or silica gel; face-up; wire.

The large flowered varieties dry beautifully, but absorb moisture readily and so are unstable and must be carefully protected and stored in an airtight container. Small flowered varieties with blooms in large panicles can be dried separately, or the entire panicle can be dried horizontally. "Quick-dry" in silica gel: 12–18 hours.

The feathery seed clusters are also interesting. Pick before overmature.

COCKSCOMB   (see *Celosia*).

COLUMBINE   (*Aquilegia*). Sand or silica gel.

It is surprising to find it possible to dry these flowers because of their unusual form, especially those with long spurs. A. *canadensis*, the native red-and-yellow American flower, and A. *alpina*, the blue Alpine flower, are lovely as are many of the hybrids.

Position for covering: Anchor the natural stem in a mound of the medium, the bloom suspended in the air with the cup tilted upward. Pour the medium to surround the flower and build up to flow into and cover as for face-up method. This dainty flower can add an interesting note to the outline and an airy quality to mass arrangements of many styles. Silica gel: 3–4 days; "quick-dry": 12–18 hours.

CROWN-OF-THORNS (*Euphorbia splendens*). Sand; face-down.

The brilliant red bracts of these small flower clusters dry with little color change and are interesting and stable.

DAFFODILS (*Narcissus*). Silica gel; face-up with stems horizontal.

Small and multiple-flowered tazetta types, such as Cheerfulness and Geranium, are attractive. Most larger kinds are very difficult. The "quick-dry" method is recommended for better texture, substance and stability. The petals are not as likely to have a thin, translucent appearance. Many are perishable under ordinary conditions of humidity. Silica gel: 3–4 days; "quick-dry": 18–24 hours.

DAHLIA. Sand or silica gel; face-up; wire, using hook.

Many types of dahlias are exceptionally beautiful as dried flowers and valuable because of their differences in form, size, pattern and wonderful colors.

All dahlias should be covered to dry when the ray petals have opened to assume their typical shape but before any disk florets in the center, or at least before two rows of disk florets, have opened. According to the Dahlia Society, overmaturity is indicated if more than two rows of pollen-bearing stamens are present. Since one of the cardinal rules for drying flowers demands that flowers must be dried before they are mature, the reason is apparent. Dahlias will drop their petals and often shatter completely if dried after they are mature.

Ball types, miniatures and pompons are most attractive and stable dried flowers, and the least inclined to drop petals.

Single, anemone and collarette types provide interesting and different forms that are delightful in arrangements but must be stored to protect them from humidity above 60 per cent.

Decorative types are often successfully dried, but the larger sizes demand special care. It is no doubt advisable to glue (see "Gluing") and use silica gel as the covering medium to reduce the drop of petals or complete shattering.

Cactus, semi-cactus and types that do not have formal petal arrangement are not generally attractive dried flowers.

Dahlia colors are fantastic in their variety and many can be expected to retain their beautiful natural hues, especially the clear peppermint pinks, yellows, lavenders, and orange reds. Some of the bi-colors and blends are exceedingly good. Color changes can be expected as noted for these colors in other flowers: pinks with a bluish cast will have the blue accentuated and dark colors will be still darker.

Very little difference in color is apparent between flowers dried by the sand or silica gel method. Both are good. Silica gel: 4–8 days; "quick-dry": 18–24 hours.

DAISY (see Gloriosa, Shasta, Gerbera, Black-eyed Susan, Michaelmas, Fever-few).

This name is often applied to flowers that have petals or ray flowers surrounding a center of disk flowers.

Daisies must be covered to dry before all the pollen-bearing stamens are present in the disk to minimize the dropping of petals. If closely examined, it can be seen that these appear row by row—beginning at the outside. If sand-dried, not more than two rows should be present, but if dried in silica gel, a few more rows can be present without danger of petal loss. When all pollen-bearing stamens are present the flower is mature. Best results are obtained when flowers are dried before this stage of development is reached.

The loss of a single petal will spoil the appearance of a daisy, and it must be glued back in place. Dip end in undiluted glue and replace.

DAY LILY (*Hemerocallis*). Silica gel; face-up.

The blooms are gone in a day and generally not stable when dried. *H. flava* (Lemon Day Lily). Will keep its shape and lovely yellow color if carefully protected from moisture.

DELPHINIUM. Sand. Spikes, horizontal; individual flowers, face-up.

D. Ajacis (Annual Delphinium) (see Larkspur).

D. Belladonna and the hybrid variety Connecticut Yankee are slender, graceful spikes of shades of blue. Silica gel is the recommended medium for covering these flowers to minimize shattering. As they dry quickly, care must be taken to prevent excessive dehydration. Silica gel: 2–4 days; "quick-dry": 8–12 hours.

Delphinium of all varieties is valued as a dried flower not only because of the colors, the size and grace of the spikes, the beauty of the individual flowers, but also because it is stable and keeps its beauty over a long period of time.

Hybrid (*D. elatum cultorum*) (Pacific Giant). These massive or slender spikes are spectacular dried flowers. The light, medium and dark blues, and mauve all dry with excellent color retention, and those with "bees" of different color are striking. If the spike is tall, the lower flowers can be cut and dried individually as they open. Then, the top of the spike can be dried with open flowers and still unopened buds at the tip for a graceful shape.

Varieties with a velvety texture have a residue that clings to their surface when they are removed from the sand. This residue should be removed by "sandblasting" (see "Grooming and Cosmetics"). Sand is the preferable medium for this variety to prevent excessive dehydration because they are quickly dried.

DEUTZIA (*D. gracilis*). Sand; horizontal.

These dainty white flowers arranged in terminal clusters on a low-growing shrub should be cut when the buds at the tip are still unopened for graceful line. These are excellent dried flowers because they remain white, are stable under average conditions, and provide dainty material for small arrangements and airy material for larger ones. Entire clusters with a few leaves are attractive.

DOCK (*Rumex crispus*). Air-dry.

Curled dock, listed as weeds according to one plant encyclopedia and surely considered so by farmers, is, however, a most useful, sturdy spike form with an interesting texture for flower arrangers. Cut them for desired color: green in late spring, rosy-beige in summer and chocolate-brown in autumn.

DOGWOOD (*Cornus florida*). Sand; face-up.

This small flowering tree is on the conservation lists and is the state flower of several states. It can be used when privately grown.

The pose and arrangement of flowers on the branches are enchanting and short branches can be dried by placing them in a horizontal position with the flowers face-up. By pouring sand in the spaces between the flowers, it can be built up to the level that will facilitate the process of covering each flower with individual care. The flowers will have a neater appearance and be more stable if they are picked and dried when the bracts open, but before the center flowers bloom. Foliage may be sand-dried or preserved in glycerine.

ECHINOPS (see Globe Thistle).

ELAEAGNUS *angustifolia* (Russian Olive). Glycerine.

The foliage of this shrub when preserved in glycerine turns to a golden-beige, but retains its silvery sheen on the underside of the leaf.

ERYNGIUM (Sea Holly). Air-dry.

Thistle-like flowers surrounded by spiny, silvery- or metallic-blue bracts, can be air-dried with little change in appearance. Hang to dry when well developed but not overmature.

EUCALYPTUS. Glycerine or evaporation.

Many varieties of this chiefly Australian, sometimes gigantic, aromatic evergreen tree are grown in California. The striking foliage is shipped to the florist market.

Many varieties are especially popular with flower arrangers because of their graceful, curving stems, leaf shapes and neutral gray-green or bluish-gray color.

Results from treatment by the glycerine method are varied because the condition of the branches when obtained are varied; they may be fresh or old, which determines whether absorption takes place completely, partially or not at all. Color changes occur according to degree of absorption and vary from gray to deep brown. When dried by the evaporation method, branches are graceful and the grayish-greenish or beige colors are appealing; however, they are more fragile than when glycerine treated.

EUPHORBIA (see Crown-of-Thorns, Flowering Spurge, Poinsettia and Snow-on-the-Mountain).

EVERLASTINGS. Air-dry.

Because the natural color and form of these chaffy or papery flowers is preserved when these flowers are air-dried, they have been used throughout the ages in many countries and are popular today. Many kinds have been improved through hybridization and can be easily grown in the garden.

The stage of development at which they are cut and hung to dry will determine their beauty and usefulness. Since some should be dried while still in bud and others when fully mature, this information will be given for each kind listed; Strawflowers, Statice, Globe Amaranth and Acroclinium.

FEVERFEW (*Chrysanthemum Parthenium*). Sand; face-down.

The single daisy type is especially attractive in mass arrangements. Entire sprays of these little flowers can be covered as described (see "Covering Techniques"). It is advisable to leave these flowers covered in the box in which they were dried until one wishes to use them, then lift individual sprays out gently by the stem. If removed and stored, the flowers become entangled and petals are knocked off.

FLOWERING SPURGE (*Euphorbia epithymoides*). Sand; face-down.

Bluish-green, small leaves with tiny flowers surrounded with bright gold bracts. Place in hot water immediately upon cutting to seal milky sap and keep from wilting.

FORGET-ME-NOT (*Anchusa* or *Myosotis*). Sand or silica gel; horizontal.

These lovely little blue flowers are attractive in miniature arrangements. The entire cluster of blooms dry quickly in silica gel: 2 days; "quick-dry": 4–6 hours.

FRUIT BLOSSOMS.

Fruit blossoms generally cannot be expected to keep their beauty in an arrangement under any but the most ideal conditions of low humidity.

FUCHSIA. Sand or silica gel; horizontal.

Silica gel will give better color for some varieties. Very typically Victorian. Tip flower so that the medium will flow into the bell. Silica gel: 3–4 days; "quick-dry": 12–18 hours.

GAZANIA. Silica gel; face-down. Wire, using hook.

Brilliant daisy-like flowers in wide range of extravagant colors. Variable results in texture and stability. The Fire Emerald is a good variety. Silica gel: 3–4 days; "quick-dry": 12–18 hours.

GERBERA DAISY (Transvaal Daisy) (see Daisy). Sand or silica gel; wire.

Many new hybrid varieties offer flowers of different colors, sizes and petal shapes and arrangement. Single flowers can be dried face-down and are most attractive. Silica gel: 3–4 days; "quick-dry": 12–18 hours.

GEUM. Silica gel; face-up.

Small double flowers of yellow and red. Seem to have better substance when dried in silica gel: 2–3 days; "quick-dry" 8–12 hours.

GLADIOLUS. Sand or silica gel; horizontal.

The "florist glads," or decorative types, do not dry to retain a pleasing textural quality. The petals become thin and translucent in appearance and collapse under all but the most favorable conditions. "Early flowering gladioli," however, are very attractive and useful dried flowers. These are reminiscent of those seen in the flower paintings of the seventeenth-century painter at the French Court of Louis XIV, Jean-Baptiste Monnoyer.

These dainty flowers on wiry stems can be grown from corms planted in the garden in the autumn.

G. *byzantinus* is beautiful in the garden; rosy-purple indicates a color change when dried.

G. *Colvillei* (The Bride) is a lovely white variety that forces well and can be found in the florist shops in March.

G. *nanus* (Peach Blossom) should be lovely color when dried. Silica gel: 3–4 days; "quick-dry": 12–18 hours.

GLOBE AMARANTH (*Gomphrena globosa*) (see Everlastings). Air-dry.

This Everlasting should be picked to dry when fully mature. Popular colors are purple, white, pink and variegated. An especially beautiful variety is G. *Haagena aurea* which has red bracts and yellow florets combined in rich orange effect.

GLOBE THISTLE (*Echinops*). Air-dry.

These metallic-blue round heads must be picked for the beauty of their bracts before they bloom. If picked later, the heads will shatter when dried. Globe Thistles are valuable in arrangements because of their perfect ball form and their gray-green and blue colors. Long stems, which are sturdy and useful, are often interestingly curved.

GLORIOSA DAISY (*Rudbeckia*) (see Daisy). Sand; face-down.

Large single daisy-like flowers in shades of gold and yellow, some zoned with mahogany-red, and others bi-color in mahogany and gold. Mahogany colors dry darker but are handsome. They must be carefully stored so that petals will not become bent (see "Storing").

GOLDEN-GLOW (*Rudbeckia laciniata hortensia*). Sand; face-up.

This is a yellow double-flowered variety. May shatter and require gluing.

GOLDENROD (*Solidago sp.*). Air-dry.

There are 140 species of Goldenrod, most from the New World. S. *canadensis* is a very graceful species for use in arrangements. Generally, those blooming in August and early September have a better appearance and lasting quality than those blooming later in the season. These often blow and shatter.

Pick when fully developed. Select carefully to avoid overmaturity when the florets at the tips turn brown. The florets do not open further after being picked or during the drying process.

GOMPHRENA (see Globe Amaranth).

GRAINS. Air-dry or glycerine.

Cut and hang at different stages for differences in color from green to beige to brown. Wheat and barley are popular for some styles of mass arrangements. The coarser, larger, bolder forms of such grains as millet and sorghum are useful for modern styles.

GRAPEVINE. Sand; horizontal.

Young shoots with new leaves and tendrils are very delicate, airy and attractive. Mature leaves can be sand-dried and pressed.

GRASSES. Air-dry.

Some are attractive because of plumes and others for seed heads. These can be gathered from the fields and roadside, and certain ornamental kinds which can be grown in the garden are listed in seed catalogues. Hang to dry when the desired color is reached and before fully mature. Cut with long stems. Blades will assume intriguing curls and curving lines when they dry. The entire feathery, silky plumes of Pampas Grass (*Cortaderia*) can be used or it may be separated into smaller airy, dainty plumes which can be secured on a wire with floral tape.

GROUNDSEL BUSH or GROUNDSEL TREE (*Baccharis halimifolia*). Air-dry.

This shrub grows in brackish marshes from New England to Texas. When branches are picked in bud in October the white flower clusters burst open showing a flash of silver as they dry. Very effective airy material, especially for use in silver containers.

GUELDER ROSE   (see Snowball).

GYPSOPHILA   (see Baby's Breath).

HEATHERS (*Calluna*) and HEATHS (*Erica*). Air-dry or evaporation.

These are small flowers in spike form; pink and rose colors.

HELIANTHUS (Sunflower). Sand; face-up; wire.

Flowers are large, mostly shades of yellow. (Also see Sunflower.)

HELICHRYSUM   (see Strawflower).

HELIOTROPE. Sand or silica gel; horizontal.

Lovely tiny flowers of deep blue or purple in flat clusters. Separate clusters into graceful sprays and cover in horizontal position. Best color with silica gel. "Quick-dry" method: 6–8 hours; silica gel: 1–2 days.

HELIPTERUM (Everlasting)   (see Acroclinium). Air-dry.

H. Sandfordii. Clusters of small pale-yellow flowers. Pick while in bud.

HELLEBORUS (Christmas Rose or Lenten Rose). Sand or silica gel.

Individual bloom face-up; multiple flower clusters stem horizontal with faces tilted up.

H. niger (Christmas Rose). Large single bell-like white flowers fading to pink.

H. orientalis atrorubens (Lenten Rose). The flowers are chocolate-purple tinted on the outside, while on the inside they are greenish, shot with purple.

These flowers are easily dried, and add interesting form and color to arrangements. They are stable and long-lasting. Silica gel: 2–3 days; "quick-dry": 8–12 hours.

HERBS. These can be hung to dry and tucked into arrangements for the delight of their fragrance. A few favorites are listed below, but there could be many additions.

Lavender (*Lavandula spica*). Pick when in bloom about midsummer.

Myrrh or Sweet Cicely (*Myrrhis odorata*). These graceful branches can be picked when the inconspicuous flowers are in bud or full bloom. They can be used in arrangements not only for their fragrance but as airy transitional material.

Rosemary (*Rosmarinus officinalis*). May grow up to 6 feet tall bearing heavily scented leaves and flowers.

Sage (*Salvia officinalis*).

Scented geranium foliage (*Pelargonium*).

Thyme (*Thymus vulgaris*).

HOLLY (*Ilex*). Glycerine.

Holly is not a personal choice except for those without spiny-toothed leaves.

I. glabra (Inkberry or winterberry). A native of eastern North America, has oblongish leaves 1 to 2½ inches, and is most attractive foliage for use in small and medium-size arrangements.

HOLLYHOCK (*Althaea rosea*). Sand or silica gel; face-up.

Interesting array of colors and forms. Some appear like satin and others like crepe paper when dried.

Individual flowers should be wired, using hook technique. Tip of stalk with several buds and one or two flowers can be attractive. Cover in horizontal position. "Quick-dry": 12–18 hours; silica gel: 3–4 days.

HONESTY (*Lunaria biennis*).

The seed pods of this plant are flattened, partitioned disks. Hang when pods are ripe. Outside coverings can be slipped off between the fingers to reveal the shining silver disks.

HONEYSUCKLE (*Lonicera*). Sand; horizontal.

Flowers and graceful curving tips of vines can be dried but are very brittle and easily broken. (See Vines.)

HOSTA (Funkia or Plantain Lily). Sand or silica gel; horizontal.

Unopened flower spikes of some varieties offer another interesting form. Silica gel: 4–5 days; "quick-dry": 18–24 hours.

Leaves preserved by evaporation or glycerine methods assume grotesque forms and become beige in color.

HYACINTH. Silica gel or sand; horizontal; wire.

The flowers of these bulbous plants are an interesting addition for use in arrangements of many styles. The flowers dry with interesting color and good texture in silica gel. When dried in sand, flowers have a translucent appearance. Stems are best supported by inserting the wire almost the entire length of the stem. Silica gel: 5–6 days; "quick-dry": 24–30 hours.

HYDRANGEA.

H. macrophylla. Sand; air-dry only at mature stage.

This will be recognized as the "florist" hydrangea, widely called *H. hortensia*. In the garden it certainly belongs among the showiest of summer- and autumn-flowering small shrubs. When grown in acid soil their colors are of various shades of blue, but pink in alkaline soil. Color changes occur during the entire flowering season. The shades are pale and delicate at first, becoming more intense as the flower develops. In late summer the clusters turn aqua or green, and in autumn are tinged with red. Each and all of these colors are useful, and all the blues are especially valuable.

Pick to dry at all different stages for the color desired and, of course, when a particularly pleasing color is available. Usually the clusters of flowers must be covered with sand to retain the lovely form of each flower. It is only in late autumn that the petals have sufficient substance and rigidity to retain their form and not collapse during the drying process. At this stage just pick and hang to air-dry.

Position for covering: Place face-down in a box with a light layer of sand in the bottom. The large clusters can be separated and placed close together to fill the box. Cover by pouring sand gently into the center of the cluster and into any spaces between them to build up the sand evenly until all are completely covered.

Drying at room temperature produces good color.

These flowers have many uses. They are especially valuable as transitional and filler material for use in mass arrangements. The entire cluster may be used, or it can be separated into smaller clusters of various sizes and the individual flower itself can be used in small bouquets.

H. paniculata grandiflora (Peegee). Air-dry.

Large flower clusters of white are produced on this shrub in late summer. As the flowers mature they change to a lovely pale-green color and then to a bronzy-pink. They need only to be picked and hung or laid to dry to keep their green or bronzy-pink color and pleasing form. The large clusters can be separated to be used as transitional and filler material in arrangements of many styles.

IRIS. Silica gel; face-up; wire.

The bulbous Dutch Iris can be successfully dried. Colors are somewhat muted, but the interesting form is happily used in some styles of arrangements. They must be carefully stored (see "Storing") in an upright position to protect them from being bent and from humidity above 55 per cent for they are not stable. Silica gel: 3–4 days; "quick-dry": 12–18 hours. (See "Covering Techniques"—Special Positions.)

IVY (*Hedera Helix*). Sand; evaporation; glycerine.

Ivy can be dried in sand to retain the grace of a short spray. It can sometimes be dried to keep its natural form by the evaporation method of preserving foliage. Mature lengths of vine can be preserved by the glycerine method. Split ends and stand in solution.

LAMBS-EARS (*Stachys lanata*). Air-dry.

Entire spray may be hung or placed in horizontal position. Leaves may be stroked with the fingers the first day or two, before they become brittle for a more natural or pleasing appearance.

LANTANA. Sand or silica gel.

Rings of tiny flowers make these small clusters interesting in small arrangements or as airy material in larger arrangements. Short sprays with buds and a few leaves or individual flowers on short stems can be dried in horizontal position with flowers face-up. Bright jewel colors of yellow and orange, pink and lavender are lovely. Silica gel: 2–3 days; "quick-dry": 8–12 hours. Less shattering with silica gel.

LARKSPUR (*Delphinium Ajacis*). Sand; horizontal.

This is one of the best spike-form flowers for dried arrangements. They are easily dried with exceptionally good form. The clear colors— blues, pinks, purples and lilac—dry with little color change and keep their color well over a long period of time. The whites stay white. For a most graceful spike, pick to dry with unopened buds at the tip.

These flowers are pretty in the garden and are easily grown from seed planted in August or from October to earliest spring.

Stems of larkspur dried separately are extremely useful as substitute stems to camouflage wires when making arrangements. Not only are larkspur stems sturdy, but also hollow and attractive, keeping their green color well. Dry different lengths and sizes of stems as they are available when the flower is cut or when the plant is removed from the bed. To dry— remove the foliage and spread out on newspaper in a dry, dark place.

LILAC (*Syringa*). Sand; horizontal.

S. vulgaris and its French hybrids are enchanting in arrangements of many styles. The thyrses are more graceful if picked to dry before the buds at the tip are open. Some varieties dry with wonderful natural color. Sometimes whites dry white, sometimes almost brown, and often white and beige mixed. These are most effective in brown and beige arrangements. Sometimes lilac colors are mixed with beige also. One could expect this color change when drying takes place in the attic during changeable springtime weather, but these color changes also take place when drying occurs in a heated house at room temperature and also with added heat. Effective use can be found for lilac of any shade. Lilac should be "sandblasted" when uncovered after they are dried. A residue clings to the underside and stems but can easily be removed by this method. If this is not done, particles of sand will continually fall after the flowers are placed in arrangements (see "Grooming and Cosmetics").

Lilac may be dried by the silica gel method, but care should be taken that it is not excessively dried which causes shrinking and fading. Silica gel: 2–3 days.

LILY (*Lilium*). Silica gel; wire.

Lilies are flamboyant and unexpected as dried flowers. The distinct forms of trumpets, pendant, sunburst, bowl and reflexed types are all exciting. Those lilies having short, broad, formal petals are more easily dried than those that are recurved and curling and narrow.

The colors obtained are varied. Many orange lilies dry with excellent natural, clear, bright color. Dotting and spotting show up well. White and pale colors often turn beige or creamy white. Pinks can be lovely or drab. All are useful depending on how they are used and combined with other colors. Those with good substance or thickness of petals generally dry with best appearance and more stable quality.

Lilies can be dried in sand but petals are sometimes broken off where they are so delicately attached to the pedicel. If the lighter weight silica gel is used, breakage is reduced. (See "Covering Techniques.") Dry lilies the day they open for best preservation of the pollen laden anthers. Store with anthers hanging straight down until ready to place in an arrangement. Protect while stored in airtight container. Silica gel: 4–5 days; "quick-dry": 18–24 hours.

LILY-OF-THE-VALLEY (*Convallaria majalis*). Silica gel or sand; horizontal.

These little bell-shaped flowers have the appearance of parchment when they dry. Silica gel: 2–3 days; "quick-dry": 8–12 hours.

LONICERA (see Honeysuckle).

LOOSESTRIFE (*Lysimachia clethroides*). Sand or silica gel; horizontal.

This narrow, goose-necked spikey white flower is a most attractive and interesting form for mass arrangements. Silica gel: 2–3 days; "quick-dry": 8–12 hours.

LOVE-IN-A-MIST (*Nigella*). Sand; face-up.

These lovely little flowers enveloped in thin green lace-like bracts are charming. The blues dry deeper blue and whites often stay white. The natural stem supports the flower adequately.

The seed pod is a most attractive inflated capsule. Pick and hang to air-dry when well developed with good green color, sometimes washed with deep purple.

LUNARIA (see Honesty).

This plant is called Honesty in England and often called Money Plant in America.

MAGNOLIA *grandiflora*.

Blossom—Silica gel; face-up.

The large cup-shaped flowers can be successfully dried in silica gel. They have the appearance of parchment. The partially open bud is most attractive and the flower should be covered to dry as soon as it opens to the desired shape. Cut at the clearly defined line where the stem changes color from green to rust. Insert a 6-inch length of 20-gauge wire. It may be necessary to increase the depth of the tin, using a soufflé collar (see "Covering Techniques"). Silica gel: 4–5 days; "quick-dry": 12–24 hours. Stays whiter if not completely dried in medium.

Foliage—Air-dry or glycerine.

Leaves are pale green or beige in color, but brittle when air-dried.

Leaves are pliable, shiny and a beautiful shade of brown when branches are preserved by the glycerine method.

Fruit—Is cone-like, rusty-woolly and heavily indented with red seeds.

Use spray glue to hold seeds in place, or dip in shellac thinned with alcohol.

Combinations of brown foliage preserved by the glycerine method, parchment-colored flowers, and the unusual fruit offer many possibilities to the modern designer.

MAHONIA (Oregon Grape Holly, *M. Aquifolium; M. Bealei*).

Foliage—Glycerine.

MAIDENHAIR FERN (*Adiantum pedatum*). Sand; face-down.

Native fern of our rocky woods. The purple-black leaf stalk from which the fern gets its name supports a whorl of fronds. A dozen whorls can be dried most satisfactorily in a box by first placing one whorl face-down on a mound of sand and then pouring sand to cover. Place the next whorl on top with the purple-black leaf stalk along side the first in a perpendicular position. Cover the fronds with sand and repeat until all are in place. These should be dried in a week to ten days at room temperature in one's work room. Remove from the sand by holding all the stems or leaf stalks in one hand and pouring the sand off. Hang the bundle or stand in a container to store.

MARGUERITE (*Chrysanthemum frutescens*) (see Daisy). Silica gel; face-down; wire.

These white or pale yellow daisy-like flowers can be dried with better substance by the "quick-dry" method (4 hours). They are not very stable and must be protected from humidity of over 55 per cent. Store to protect their form. (See "Storing.")

MARIGOLD (*Tagetes*). Sand or silica gel; face-up.

All the marigolds are good candidates for drying, and the new hybrids are more exciting each year. The small French types, from pale yellow to deepest coppery red, in solid colors and variations, are attractive and stable dried flowers. They are valuable for arrangements of Baroque style as well as for Modern. These do not require wiring before they are dried because they can be dried by placing face-up at an angle on a ridge of sand leaving about a 3-inch length of stem. The stem is hollow, so a wire can be inserted and fastened with floral tape when the flower is placed in an arrangement. Silica gel: 3–4 days; "quick-dry": 12–18 hours.

The African types offer delightful pale yellow hues and range to brilliant orange shades. Dry with a short length of stem, 3–4 inches, as above, or wire through the stem using a hook to insure against the stems' being broken because of the large size and weight of the flower. Pick marigolds when they are fully developed but before they are overmature. The green center, which is attractive in immature flowers, will turn dark and unattractive when the flower dries. Silica gel: 4–5 days; "quick-dry": 18–24 hours.

MERTENSIA   (see Virginia Blue Bells).

MICHAELMAS DAISY (Hardy Fall Aster). Sand or silica gel; face-down.
Dainty flowers of lavender, purple, rose, blue and white. Small sprays can be successfully dried if care is taken in handling and storing after they are dried to prevent petal loss. Silica gel: 2–3 days; "quick-dry": 8–12 hours.

MOCK-ORANGE (*Philadelphus*). Sand; horizontal.
Dry short sprays with flowers face-up. Do not remove all leaves.

The vast differences in the stability of flowers of different varieties is clearly demonstrated in mock-oranges. Petals of some varieties become soft and collapse after they are dried when exposed to average conditions of humidity. Others are crisp and lovely when exposed to the same conditions. Trial and error with the varieties at hand must determine those best suited for preserving. The old-fashioned common mock-orange *P. coronarius* is not a good candidate. *P. pubescens* has proved to be exceptionally stable.

MOUNTAIN LAUREL (*Kalmia latifolia*). Glycerine.
The handsome foliage of this plant can be excellently preserved by the glycerine method, and can be used to great advantage in many arrangements. The shape and size of the leaves and their graceful arrangement on the branches contribute to their beauty. This evergreen shrub is on the conservation lists.

MULLEIN (*Verbascum thapsus*). Air-dry.
Tightly bunched clusters of seeds on tall (to 6 feet) spikes have rough, coarse appearance suitable for use in some modern styles. Basal leaves are large, gray and velvety, gracefully arranged to appear as a rosette during autumn and winter. These can be air-dried by laying face-up. To retain this form may require periodic stroking and arrangement of leaves as they dry.

NIGELLA   (see Love-in-a-Mist).

ORCHID. Silica gel; face-up; wire.
Only a few varieties of these spectacular flowers have been available for experimentation. Silica gel is the medium required because of unusual shapes and substance. Silica gel: about 5 days; "quick-dry": about 24 hours.

OSMANTHUS (Tea Olive). Glycerine.
Branches of these small spiny-toothed leaves can be preserved.

PACHYSANDRA *terminalis* (Japanese Spurge). Glycerine.
Whorls of leaves of this ground cover can be preserved by splitting or crushing ends of stems and standing in glycerine solution. Some retain a green color for months, while other turn beige or brown.

PALM.
Most varieties are distinctive and noble foliage plants of the tropics.

Not only the foliage, but also the spathe and the fruit can be air-dried or collected after drying naturally to provide unusual and bold material for modern arrangements. Appreciation and imagination are the most important requirements in selection.

PANSY (*Viola tricolor hortensis*) (see *Viola cornuta*). Silica gel; face-up.

These favorite flowers are charming in dried arrangements. The natural stem is fragile when dried. Wiring is difficult. Pansies have better substance and stability when dried in silica gel by the "quick-dry" method: 12–18 hours. When these flowers are dried more slowly they have a greater tendency to absorb moisture from the air and collapse in any but the most ideal conditions of low humidity.

PEARLY EVERLASTING (*Anaphalis margaritacea*). Air-dry.

As the name implies, this wildflower resembles a cluster of pearls when it dries. The plant will often be found growing on newly scarred ground where a powerline has been laid or on the bank of a new road or in uncultivated fields. It is not a very conspicuous plant making it difficult to recognize when not in full bloom. A yellow spot at the tip of the buds shows when the optimum stage for picking has been reached (usually occurring in late August or early September), and the pearls will burst forth as the flower dries. If picked at the blooming stage, the pearls will disappointingly "blow" or shatter. These flowers make very good transitional material in arrangements.

PENTSTEMON (Beard Tongue). Sand or silica gel; horizontal.

Spike flowers with good color and interesting form. Silica gel: 3–4 days; "quick-dry": 12–18 hours. Hairy: sandblast.

PEONY (*Paeonia*). Silica gel or sand; face-up; wire.

These flowers have exceptional beauty when dried. Silica gel is the better medium. They are valuable not only for the lovely shapes of the double peonies, but also for the dramatic single flowers with prominent yellow stamens. For large arrangements, these large flowers are most welcome. The clear, light pinks, salmon pinks, whites and bright reds dry with little color change. The rosy pinks and blue-reds dry with some change of color but are generally attractive. For double flowers of irregular petal arrangement, silica gel is the better medium for preserving the natural form. Cut when open to the desired stage or cut after sepals on buds are relaxed. Place stems in warm water and allow to open in the protected environment of the house. Cover to dry when flower opens to reveal its highest beauty. Silica gel: 5–6 days; "quick-dry": 24–30 hours.

Foliage—Dried in sand preserves its interesting, natural shape and beautiful green color; it can also be preserved by the glycerine method.

PERIWINKLE (*Vinca minor*). Glycerine.

The leaves of this ground cover are small, ovalish, leathery in texture, and arranged attractively on the stem and useful for some small arrangements. Crush stems and stand in glycerine solution. When color turns to brown and one prefers green foliage for use, spray paint lightly. For black containers or black design on white, spray with black paint for artistic effect.

PHILADELPHUS (see Mock-orange).

PHYSOSTEGIA *virginiana* (Obedient Plant or False Dragonhead). Sand or silica gel; horizontal.

The trumpet-shaped flowers can be moved around on the wand-like stem, which accounts for the common name. Shape the spike as desired and place to cover. Silica gel: 3–4 days; "quick-dry": 12–18 hours.

PIERIS *japonica*. Glycerine.

Attractive branches of foliage having two years' growth will show interesting contrasts of brown shades.

POINSETTIA (*Euphorbia pulcherrima*). Sand or silica gel; face-up.

Unusual dried flowers with good red color; whites turn cream color. Silica gel: 4–5 days; "quick-dry": 18–24 hours.

POPPY (*Papaver*). Seed pods—air-dry.

QUEEN ANNE'S LACE (*Daucus carota*). Sand; face-down.

These wild flowers of the fields and roadsides are truly beautiful circles of fine lace. When dried face-down, it is possible to retain long stems which are attractive and sturdy when dried. Some stand upright during the drying process while others flop over at right angles. Since it is virtually impossible to insert a wire into most of the stems, gently lift them up before they become stiff and tape them to the sides of the box or to a strip placed across the top of a deep box.

RHODODENRON. Silica gel; face-up; wire.

The lovely large flower clusters of the hybrid rhododendrons are dramatic dried flowers. Color changes can be expected with pinks and reds, which have a bluish cast. Protection from humidity above 55 per cent is required. Store in an airtight container. Silica gel: 4–5 days; "quick-dry": 18–24 hours.

ROSE (*Rosa*). Sand or silica gel; face-up; wire; glue for sand-drying.

Roses can be dried with distinctive beauty that gives inspiration to the arranger and charm and elegance to the arrangement. This beauty is retained for a long period of time by many varieties. All stages of development from tight bud to full-blown are attractive. The exquisite form of those having *broad, widely flaring* petals can be perfectly preserved, as can single flowers. Roses having this characteristic form are to be found in all classifications or types of roses from "Roses of Yesterday" to the latest introduction of the hybridist. It is almost impossible to preserve those kinds that open with petals reflexed and rolled back into peaks.

Not only can roses be dried with natural color or expected changes (see "Color Changes"), but unexpected colors never before seen in a rose can be produced. Brilliant, vivid, clear hues, as well as soft shades, muted tones and interesting gradations can be obtained depending upon the original color of the rose, the method of preservation, or the rate of dehydration. Roses from the same bush may be amazingly different as dried flowers.

Whether or not a rose is dried to retain its natural color is not as important as the quality of its color. If it is lovely because it is bright and clear, it can be used in arrangements in which these qualities are desired. Perhaps bright red is the color best suited for the dominant one in an arrangement for a particular room, such as that in the Palladian Room at Gunston Hall. The beauty of delicate shades and muted values can be most valuable in arrangements created as decorative pieces for rooms with subtle color schemes. There is even delight in a rose that has lost most of its original color in the drying process, for a beige rose can be stunning in a brown-and-beige arrangement. Colors are often appealing because of the ways in which they are combined.

Colors are intensified when the silica gel method is used with little variation for the same variety. For the brightest, clearest colors, use silica gel. For great variety of color use the sand-drying method.

Colors and color changes expected for roses are important. White and near-whites stay white or turn cream or beige. Yellows and yellow blends are pale to deep gold. Apricots and orange and orange blends show little change in hue but changes in value. Orange-reds change to red. Light, medium and dark reds dry darker. Pastel clear pinks dry pink. Light and medium pinks with a bluish cast will have the blue accentuated and dry orchid or magenta.

Selecting and preparing roses to be dried

It is a great pleasure to select roses from one's own garden. Varieties having good substance and fine texture are the most attractive and long-lasting dried flowers. Those that have the better keeping qualities as fresh-cut flowers can be expected to be the more stable when dried. Roses of delicate substance and thin petals must be carefully protected from excessive humidity. The perfect rose is the one that should be preserved. Any imperfections are exaggerated when flowers are dried. It is important to select and dry them by both the sand and silica gel methods to produce the wide range of colors desirable for arrangements.

Roses can be cut and dried at the desired stage of development— tight bud, partially open bud or full-blown. They can also be cut after the sepals on the bud have relaxed and brought into the house to open and dry when they assume their best form. By this means they can be protected from damage by rain, insects or spray.

When cutting a rose, do it with the thought of buds to come later and in relation to the shape of the plant. Make the cut itself with a sharp knife or clippers one-fourth inch above the topmost leaf to be left on the stem. This leaf should be to the outside of the plant for a more open bush. To get more roses from the same stem, leave at least two leaves or five leaflets.

Conditioning

For best form and turgidity or crispness, cut roses in the morning after the dew has evaporated, or in late afternoon—not in the middle of a hot, sunshiny day when they will be flaccid or wilted. Place stems in warm water of at least 100 degrees.

Many varieties of roses from the florist can be successfully dried. The stems should be recut and placed in warm water until the roses are turgid and opened to the desired form.

Gluing

It is necessary to glue roses that are to be preserved by the sand-drying method. This prevents petals from dropping or being completely shattered when uncovered. This extra chore is worth the trouble to keep the natural form intact. (See "Gluing.") Gluing is not necessary when using the silica gel method, except for single roses and a few varieties at the full-blown stage.

Timing for silica gel method

3–8 days is required. The "quick-dry" method is *not* recommended because colors are not as clear. Single roses will, of course, dry fastest, while large buds need the longest drying time. It is important to prevent excessive dehydration because bright colors are less vibrant and pastels fade away.

Rose foliage can be sand-dried or preserved in glycerine. Sprays of new foliage are most attractive when sand-dried but very fragile.

RUDBECKIA   (see Gloriosa Daisy).

SALVIA.

S. farinacea (Blue salvia). Air-dry.

These are valuable because the spikes are slender and often gracefully curved, as well as for the powder-blue or silver colors.

S. splendens (Scarlet Sage). Air-dry or sand.

Well known red color dries with little change. The jewel-toned colors available should not be overlooked—purple, pinks, white and variegated. These flowers can be air-dried with good form when mature. The individual flowers are easily broken from the spike when dried. The immature tips can have good form when dried in sand; horizontal position.

SARCOCOCCA *hookeriana humilis.* Glycerine.

An evergreen shrub with oblong pointed leathery leaves, about 1 to 1½ inches long. Graceful small branches most useful for many kinds of arrangements.

SCARLET SAGE   (see *Salvia*).

SCOTCH BROOM   (*Cystisus scoparius*). Air-dry.

The slender green branches of this shrub can be curved into the desired shape by manipulation—curving gently by stroking, or even by tying loosely and hanging to dry.

SHASTA DAISY (*Chrysanthemum maximum*) (see Daisy). Sand; face-down; wire.

When these single flowers are dried before any of the disk flowers in the center are open, shrinking causes cracks and the attractive close-packed appearance is lost. The charm of the daisy form may compensate for this minor flaw. If the center disk flowers are open before the daisy is dried, then petals tend to drop. Gluing at this stage—before drying—may solve the problem. (See "Gluing.") New hybrid varieties, especially those with high-crested centers, are of interesting form.

SNAPDRAGON (*Antirrhinum majus*). Sand or silica gel; horizontal.

The spike form and interesting shape and wonderful colors of the new hybrids are as useful in dried arrangements as fresh. Those varieties of typical form must have each floret snapped open or gently pulled open as it is covered to allow some sand to flow into the pocket so that it will not be flat when dried.

Bright Butterflies and other varieties having an open face make the process of covering simpler.

Snapdragons have hairy stems and calyx to which any covering medium clings. This can be removed by "sandblasting" (see "Grooming and Cosmetics") and also by rubbing the stem with the handle of a water-color paint brush. The tips of snaps will droop if the arrangement is exposed to humidity in excess of 60 per cent.

SNOWBALL (*Viburnum opulus*). Sand or silica gel; face-down.

This is the "guelder rose" of the seventeenth and eighteenth centuries and can be used with good effect in mass arrangements in the styles of that era. The round clusters of white flowers do resemble a snow-ball as the common name applies. Pick before the flowers are well developed for better substance and stability when the flowers are dried. Silica gel: 3–4 days; "quick-dry": 12–18 hours.

SNOW-ON-THE-MOUNTAIN (*Euphorbia marginata*). Sand; horizontal.

Branches can be dried for the pale green-and-white margined leaves, along with the showy, white bracts of the flower clusters.

STATICE (see Everlasting). Air-dry.

S. Bonduellii (yellow) and *S. caspia* (lavender), called Sea Lavender, are airy sprays.

S. sinuata sprays hold compact clusters of stiff papery flowers of many colors, including purple, lavender, blue, pink, rose, apricot, yellow and white. The stems fade and can be touched up with green spray paint, if desired. (See "Grooming and Cosmetics.")

STEMS.

Natural stems that are hollow and sturdy should be saved or dried separately for use as substitute stems to camouflage wires or to increase length of short-stemmed flowers as required for arrangements. Strip off leaves and side stems as required and lay in a dry, dark place until dry. Stems of various sizes and lengths, colors and curves will be required. Suggested: Prince's feather celosia, day lily, larkspur, delphinium, feverfew.

STOCK or GILLIFLOWER (*Matthiola incana*). Sand or silica gel; horizontal.

Spikes of double-rosette-type flowers of many colors dry with good form. White stays white, or some flowers interestingly shaded to beige. Not all natural colors are retained (see "Color Changes"). These flowers are not stable except under low conditions of humidity. Silica gel: 3–4 days; "quick-dry": 18–24 hours.

STRAWFLOWER (*Helichrysum*). Air-dry; wire.

One of the best known of the everlastings. They can be easily grown in the garden. The new hybrids are a spectrum of colors and bright in arrangements, especially since the petals have a sheen that reflects the light. The small garden-grown strawflowers add interest to arrangements without being as dominant as the large florist types. Pick for drying after the sepals have released their hold on the bud, but before one-half open, as they continue to open while drying. Pick each flower as soon as it reaches the desired stage leaving the others to develop. (Large flowers can be produced by disbudding.) Since the natural stem will not support the flower in an arrangement, causing the heads to droop, they should be wired before drying. (See "Wiring.") It is sometimes possible to insert the wire through a stem of sufficient length so that no further camouflage of the wire is required when the flower is used in the arrangement. Although these stems are not easily wired, a short stem will provide a means of holding the flower so as not to mutilate it while the wire is being inserted. The stem shrinks to hold the wire securely. If the wire is pushed too far into the head it will protrude when the flower is dried. Stand in a container with the heads free, not touching, and dry at room temperature.

SUMAC (*Rhus*). Air-dry.

The showy fruiting clusters and brilliant red foliage are attractive in the autumn. The compound leaves can be pressed to preserve their bright red color, but are easily broken when dried. Cut the handsome fruits when they are almost mature but still show some of the bronze color, as well as when they are deep red in color. The smaller clusters can be used in mass arrangements. Remember that long stems may be useful for Modern styles.

SUNFLOWER (*Helianthus giganteus*). Air-dry.

The seed head of this plant can be as much as a foot in diameter. The pattern of the head with the seeds is interesting and equally so if the seeds have been shelled out or if the birds have feasted on them. This is unusual bold material for the modern designer.

SWEET PEA (*Lathyrus odoratus*). Silica gel.

These flowers are coming back into style and not considered so insipid or sentimental as not to be useful by the sophisticate. New varieties provide flowers of sufficient substance to be dried successfully. They must be protected from humidity.

L. latifolia (Perennial Sweet Pea). This variety can be dried in sand or silica gel. Color change occurs which is pleasing—from blue-pink to lavender. Silica gel: 2–3 days.

TRANSVAAL DAISY (see *Gerbera*).

TRUMPET-VINE (*Campsis radicans*). Sand; horizontal.

This foliage is attractive with leaflets arranged feather fashion with an odd one at the end. Tips of the vine curve gracefully and it is valuable for its dainty, airy effect.

TULIP (*Tulipa*). Silica gel; face-up; wire.

Tulips surely deserve their great popularity. Because of their characteristic form and beautiful color, they are dramatic when dried and are used and seen in arrangements with the greatest pleasure.

Pick to dry as soon as they show their best form as they then have better substance and stability. Although they can be dried in sand, there is less danger of breaking off the petals when uncovering if they are dried in silica gel. Silica gel: 4–5 days; "quick-dry": 18 hours.

It is not necessary to remove the center as suggested by Ferrari in the seventeenth century and by the article in *The American Museum* for December 1738.

VERBENA (*Vervain*). Sand or silica gel; face-up.

Rings of small flowers surrounding unopened buds in the center are an attractive form. White stays white, pinks, coral, red, purple, blue and amethyst are all lovely colors. Those with a white eye add brightness to an arrangement. Silica gel: 3–4 days; "quick-dry": 12–18 hours.

VIBURNUM. Sand.

V. *Burkwoodi*, V. *carlcephalum* and V. *Carlesi*. The domed clusters of these flowers can be dried face-up or face-down. Pick with a few leaves when flowers first open. These provide a different form.

VINCA MINOR (see Periwinkle).

VINES.

Many kinds of vines, such as wisteria, grape and honeysuckle, are popular for designs of contemporary styles. They are used in natural form or peeled, and may also be manipulated into any desired shape by being soaked in water until they are pliable then curved and tied until they dry. Sometimes these vines are painted for a different effect.

VIOLA *cornuta* (Viola and Johnny Jump-Up). Sand or silica gel; face-up.

The new hybrids are a color carnival, not as large as pansies but more stable when dried. These flowers bloom in profusion in the spring garden. The Johnny jump-ups have diminutive pansy charm. Silica gel: 2–3 days; "quick-dry": 8–12 hours.

VIRGINIA BLUE BELLS (*Mertensia virginica*). Silica gel; horizontal.

The entire cluster of these funnel-shaped bells is dainty and a clear sky-blue color when dried. Silica gel: 2–3 days; "quick-dry": 8–12 hours.

ZINNIA. Sand; face-up or face-down; wire, using hook.

Zinnias are the big exception to the general rule of picking flowers when they are first opened. Allow them to develop before picking and drying. After the flower first opens additional rows of petals develop and the flower increases in depth. Varieties that have wide petals, rather than the cactus or curly types, will have good shape when dried because of their definitely delineated form. The great variety of zinnias of many sizes and colors and forms provide many possibilities for use in arrangements. The mammoth flowered zinnias can be used in large arrangements. They are of bold form and color, which is often required. The little button varieties and the medium sizes provide such a great spread of colors. Just as there is such a wide color range in zinnias, so is there a definite change in color when the flowers are dried. Some reds change to rust or purple during the drying process or upon exposure to light; some oranges change to pink. Store the flowers so they will have exposure to light and the major color change will have taken place before they are placed in an arrangement.

Crested zinnias are a variety that has recently been introduced. They have high cushion centers, surrounded by broad petals and come in a great variety of colors. These are interesting to use because of their different form.

The Persian Carpet variety, which comes in jewel colors with each petal edged in a light color, adds interest to a collection of dried flowers.

The Mexicana or Old Mexico zinnia is deep red edged with sharp yellow and is excellent.

Zinnias are easily dried. They are sturdy flowers that last well in arrangements. The large and medium sizes must be stored so that they will not rest on their sides, in which case the petals will become bent under their own weight. (See "Storing.")

Wire zinnias before drying because their hollow stems are not sturdy and will collapse during the drying process or break when being placed in an arrangement. Sand is much the best medium in which to dry because they dry quickly and keep their natural appearance. Care must be used with silica gel because excessive dehydration results in burned petal edges, shrinkage and color streaking.

The larger flowers should be dried face-down. When they are dried face-up, they tend to cave in at the center.

The little button type can be dried face-up or face-down. If there is a feature on the face of the flower you wish to preserve, such as the little yellow disk florets, dry face-up.

The medium-size zinnias can be dried face-up or face-down, depending on the shape of each flower. The concave flowers are placed face-down over a cone of sand; the crested zinnia, face-up so that they can be covered without changing form. The Mexicana or Persian Carpet should be dried face-up or in diagonal position because the petals radiate separately, and this feature should be preserved.

Watch the color changes that take place with reds, pinks and oranges and use them to good advantage. Yellows fade, and whites turn beige.

Index